London's Water

Timber Wharves — Hertford Union Canal

London's Waterway Guide

A Complete Guide to the Rivers and Canals of Greater London

Compiled and Written by
Chris Cove - Smith

Imray Laurie Norie and Wilson Ltd

Published by
Imray Laurie Norie and Wilson Ltd
Wych House St Ives Cambridgeshire

2nd Edition 1986
1st Edition 1977

Caution
While every effort has been made to check and cross check the data and information given in this book the Author and Publisher cannot accept responsibility for any accidents, injury or damage occasioned by the use of this information or data.

British Library Cataloguing in Publication Data.

Cove-Smith, Chris
   London's waterway guide. – 2nd ed.
   1. Inland navigation – England – London
   – Handbooks, manuals, etc.
   I. Title
   914.21'04858   HE436

   ISBN 0-852881-04-5

Printed at The Bath Press, Avon

Contents

Contents

Foreword

In 1986, two important events happened on the Thames tideway. In the first place Thames Water took over the GLC duties on the river including the management of the great Thames Barrier. Secondly Chris Cove-Smith decided to update his splendid London's Waterway Guide.

It is a pleasure and a privilege to be asked to write this brief foreword. I have known Chris for a great many years and always admired his meticulous knowledge of London's waterways. In this book he opens the path for so many of us who are canal lovers to explore the tideway and also for those of us who are yachtsmen to plunge into that mysterious world of canal locks and tunnels.

London's waterways comprise a fascinating ring of tidal river and inland canals and, if we are to enjoy them fully, then we must be able to understand the intricacies of both tidal and non-tidal navigation.

Today more and more narrow boats are slipping out from Limehouse Basin and going up river under the great bridges of London and returning to the canal system through the links at Brentford, Reading or Oxford. I hope too that more of the smaller yachts will try the reverse course and learn the magic of London's hidden waterways, mooring perhaps one night in St. Katharines Dock and the next in Little Venice. From there they may go on as my wife, June, and I have done to range far and wide into the waterways of France, Germany and Switzerland and ultimately, we hope, Berlin and Ankara! Certainly last year armed with Chris Cove-Smith's splendid book we passed happily down the estuary and out into the North Sea and across to Calais and on to the head waters of the Rhine in Switzerland.

Truly this book is not just a guide to London's waterways but for the 20,000 yachtsmen on the upper river it can prove a gateway to Europe. I do most strongly recommend it.

John Humphries
Wimbledon
1986

Acknowledgements

I wish to acknowledge the enormous amount of help I have been given by the officers of the navigation and other authorities consulted, in particular those mentioned below, in addition to the boat builders, barge owners, marina operators and boat hirers, publicans and restaurateurs — all of whom offered advice and valuable information.

The charts were checked from afloat by teams from the National Westminster Bank Sailing Club, the two research boats being *NatWester I* and *NatWester III*. The teams, many of whom supplied information for this second edition, were:

Christopher Brearey	Dick Hunt
Brian Butcher	Roy Manning
Donald Carter	Roger Manning
Bernard Cordingley	Brian Turrell
Frank Greenhow	Brian Vallancey
Richard Hering	Tom White
Jane Hering	Graham Woodman

I must also thank Bill, Gloria and Susan Jones of the same club, who assisted me most expertly with the proofreading of the first edition; and my wife, Audrey Cove-Smith and daughter, Sally Cove-Smith for the same services with the second.

I am also indebted to the following officers of the various authorities consulted for their helpful suggestions and corrections:

British Waterways Board Anthony Grantham, MBE; Frances Moon; Pat Hendrick; Michael Jiggins; and Bill Beak; and for the second edition: Anna Ellis; Graham Avory; Frances Read; Bob Cotton; John Carr; and Jack Butler.

Port of London Authority Capt. Douglas Dear; Graham Avory; and Andrew Britter; and for the second edition: Capt. Tony Bull; Capt. Mike Bealey; Capt. Tony Williams; Terry Hatton; and Capt. Keith Hendon.

Greater London Council Robin Hales; and for the second edition: Maurice Hudson.

Thames Water Authority Paul Beverstock and Mike Taylor, in respect of the second edition.

London Regional Transport Kenneth Pope.

Metropolitan Police, Thames Division John Joslin. In the second edition considerable information has been provided from this excellent source following my appointment as a Special Constable of the Division. I am indebted to Supt. M. E. Allen; Chief Inspector C. Patchett; Inspector C. Chapman; Commandant John Hicks; and PC's Kevin Keefe, Danny Lines and Ken Wood. My thanks also go to my Skippers John Mate and Gerry Western and crew colleagues, WSC Vivien Newton; SC Colin Hardware; and SC Doug Redfern as well as many of the crews of Thames Specials with whom I have been on patrol.

A number of members of the Inland Waterways Association, including Frederic Doerflinger, David Wood, Bob Shopland and Paul Winch provided useful additional information and encouragement, as did Anthony Reed, then Director of the Thames Information Centre.

In the second edition considerable additional material was gathered for me by David and Elizabeth Wood, Ron Bingham and Len House.

I must also thank Derek Pratt who took some of the photographs, not only for these but also for answering many of my queries from his knowledge of the area, gained from his hefty mileage walking most of the towpaths.

Most of the numerous sources of reference are contained in the bibliography.

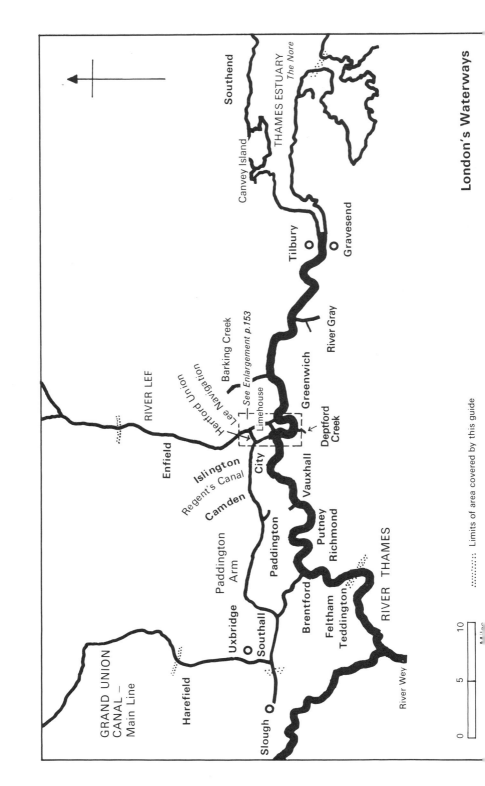

London's Waterways

GRAND UNION CANAL – Main Line

Harefield

Uxbridge

Southall

Slough

Paddington Arm

Paddington

Camden

Islington
Regent's Canal

Enfield

RIVER LEF

RIVER LEE

Hertford Union
Lee Navigation

Barking Creek

See Enlargement p.153

Limehouse

City

Vauxhall

Brentford

Putney
Richmond

Feltham
Teddington

RIVER THAMES

River Wey

Greenwich

Deptford Creek

River Gray

Tilbury

Gravesend

THAMES ESTUARY
The Nore

Canvey Island

Southend

.... Limits of area covered by this guide

0   5   10
Miles

Introduction

GENERAL

This guide deals with three main types of waterway — firstly, the tidal river, secondly, the canal or canalised river having little or no current and thirdly, the navigable river with canal sections, which has considerable current caused by rain and storm drainage.

The River Thames as depicted in charts 1 to 20 is fully tidal from Richmond downstream and partly tidal between Teddington and Richmond. Tidal constants are given at various points, the figures showing the hours and minutes after (+) or before (−) High Water Springs, Low Water Springs, High Water Neaps and Low Water Neaps in that order, at London Bridge which is known as the Standard Port. Times of High and Low Water at London Bridge are published annually by the Admiralty in tables of tidal predictions as well as by a number of other almanac publishers, although for the purposes of the small-boat owner, figures based on the Admiralty tables published daily by the national press are perfectly adequate. More details of tides and how they affect navigation of the river will be found in the preambles to Sections 1 to 4.

Masters of craft who intend to navigate in the Tideway should be absolutely certain that their craft have the necessary power to stem the tide should this be necessary, either in an emergency, or if they deliberately need to travel against the stream. The average speed of the current varies between 2 and 4 knots and, except where noted on the charts, tends to be faster on the outside of bends and where the channel narrows. A further point to watch is that at about half-tide when the stream is running at its fastest there may be considerable differences in level on either side of a bridge span, especially where a bridge is constructed with short spans and thick piers.

The height and speed of the tide also depends to a large extent on the amount of water being discharged from the upper river over the weir at Teddington. This factor may also serve to vary the true time of High or Low Tide. Tidal predictions are based on an average daily flow of 400,000,000 gallons at Teddington Weir. Allowances are also made for the considerable quantity of treated effluent discharged at Isleworth and other sewage works in the Tideway.

Between Teddington and Richmond (Half-tide) Lock (Charts 1 to 3) the river rises to a High Tide level from about two hours before, and falls again for two hours after, at which time the level is prevented from falling further by the insertion of overhead sluice gates at Richmond Footbridge. This procedure maintains adequate depth for navigation in the reaches above Richmond. In order to pass these sluices during the period of Low Tide below the footbridge, craft have to lock out of this Section by means of Richmond Lock, details of which are given in Section 1.

Besides covering the Thames from Teddington to Margaret Ness, the guide also covers the Grand Union Canal (Main Line) as far as the former GLC boundary just north of the point at which Springwell Lane crosses it near Rickmansworth. Returning to Bull's Bridge Junction on the main line the whole of the Paddington Arm is included as well as the Regent's Canal which joins this arm at Little Venice to the Thames again by way of the Limehouse Basin (Regent's Canal Dock), at Poplar. The two connections to the Lee Navigation, the Hertford Union (or Duckett's) Canal and the Limehouse Cut (which is partly tidal) are also shown.

The final waterway covered, the Lee Navigation, is an improved river, an original watercourse that was probably first used for navigation in Roman times. It is believed that a pound lock was first constructed at Waltham towards the end of the sixteenth century and in subsequent centuries various improvements to the navigation between Hertford and Bow Creek were made to accommodate larger and larger craft. Locks were built, tortuous meanders were by-passed by canal sections and weirs constructed. Early in the twentieth century the present locks were widened and paired up to Enfield to assist the timber trade, and navigators should note that this waterway still enjoys commercial status under the 1968 Transport Act.

Any lighter traffic should be given precedence, but very little now may be encountered, as far up as Ponders End, the last mechanised lock. The locks at Enfield and above are all manually operated and the river becomes more tranquil and rural. Since the Lee is essentially a natural river, flooding is possible. Current speeds are therefore variable as also are the depths and headrooms of bridges. Careful attention should be paid to the text of Section 8 on this subject.

Bow Creek is, in fact, the estuary of the Lee and is tidal. Note that passage is not normally recommended at Low Tide. High Water Springs occurs at Bow Locks near Bromley at about the same time as at London Bridge. The charts in this guide finish at Waltham Town Lock.

The River Thames has also been shown seawards from the junction with Bow Creek. Navigation seawards is best not attempted by other than sea-going craft which should make use of *Reed's Almanac,* Imray's Charts *C2, C1* and *Y18* or the relevant Admiralty Charts *(2484* and *1185)* although use may be made of the six charts in Part IV (Section 9).

The River Thames above Teddington is charted on Stanford's *River Thames Map* and Nicholson's *Ordnance Survey Guide to the River Thames* and in the Link House Publication's *Thames Book,* revised and republished annually. Continuations northward of the Grand Union Canal (Main Line) and the Lee Navigation are contained in Nicholson's *Ordnance Survey Guide to the Waterways* (Volume 1 — *South*), although the information is shown at a smaller scale than this present volume. Imray's map, *Inland Waterways of England and Wales* is also useful.

Handling
Complete notes on handling are contained in specialist works on the subject, such as my *Beginners Guide to Motor Cruising* or, for the more advanced skipper, *Pilotage on Inland Waterways* by R. E. Chase and myself both of which, un-

fortunately, are now out of print but can be borrowed from major public libraries. Particular note should be paid to the special requirements for the canals. Winding points for narrow boats and barges are shown on the charts, but owing to silting and neglect this does not necessarily mean that they are still dredged to full depth right across.

Craft not specifically designed for canal work may encounter problems by virtue of the low speed limit (4 mph), particularly those having reduction gears and large diameter propellers. Continual helm correction may be required to counteract the athwartship thrust of a single screw installation. Weed and rubbish clearance may also be a problem for craft, which unlike the modern narrow cruisers, are not fitted with a weed hatch.

All craft should be equipped with an adequate 'shaft' or 'quant pole', preferably sturdier than the ubiquitous boat hook, for getting out of trouble or off the mud. At least two such shafts are the usual complement of the narrow-boat proper.

LIST OF CHARTS

Mileages shown on the charts are taken from *Bradshaw's Canals and Navigable Rivers of England and Wales* compiled by H. R. de Salis (1904 edition), except those for the River Thames which are based on tables supplied by the Port of London Authority. Scales are approximate only at 5 inches to 1 mile on the main charts. Widths of streets and canals have been increased in many cases for clarity. Tracks and footpaths shown on the charts do not necessarily imply that they are rights of way. All charts have been drawn by the author and are based upon the Ordnance Survey Map with the sanction of the Controller of Her Majesty's Stationery Office, Crown Copyright Reserved.

The Charts are grouped in sequence and are to be found on pages as follows:

Part IV

Grand Union Canal (Main Line)

Grand Union Canal (Paddington Arm)

Regent's Canal

Lee Navigation

Inset Maps

Key Map

Detail Charts

Notes The banks of the River Thames as viewed proceeding downstream — left and right — have always taken the names of the counties in which they were formerly located since the river itself formed the boundary.

Thus the left bank is termed the Middlesex Bank as far as Bow Creek and the right bank is termed the Surrey Bank as far as Thamesmead. Thereafter the banks are termed Essex Bank and Kent Bank respectively.

The terms *North* and *South* are only approximate and in some cases are obviously confusing since they are strictly inaccurate.

The term *South Bank* is used but is normally only accepted to mean that part of the Surrey Bank which lies between Lambeth and Tower Bridges.

WEATHER FORECASTING

Weather forecasts for the London Area are available by recorded messages provided by the telephone service. The number to ring is (for London) 01-246 8091.

Personal advice by the Meteorological Office is also given to members of the public on 01-836 4311.

PUBLIC TRANSPORT INFORMATION

Railway (British Rail and London Transport Underground) stations are shown on the charts and bus route numbers are shown along all main roads, with certain exceptions in the central London areas.

Bus route terminals are shown by means of a box with the relevant route numbers inserted. Locations of these are only approximate.

At the end of each Section of this guide are tabulated lists of railway stations and routes of buses. In the case of railway stations an indication of the main route, region and approximate service frequency is given.

Rail

Details of rail services were correct as supplied by British Rail and London Regional Transport at the time of going to press, although the information was supplied 'subject to alterations and cancellations without notice'.

Enquiries concerning rail services should be directed as follows:

Southern Region (all terminals)	— Tel: 01-928 5100
Eastern Region (except King's Cross)	— Tel: 01-283 7171
Eastern Region (King's Cross only)	— Tel: 01-837 3355
Midland Region	— Tel: 01-387 7070
Western Region	— Tel: 01-262 6767
Underground	— Tel: 01-222 1234

For written or personal enquiries, you may contact the enquiry offices at the respective main-line terminals or the central British Rail information and booking centre at Lower Regent Street, London SW1. London Transport Underground enquiry offices are located at certain central London Underground interchange stations for personal enquiries, while written enquiries should be made to the Public Relations Officer, London Regional Transport, 55, Broadway, London SW1H 0BD.

Bus

London Regional Transport Buses in Sections 3 and 7 run at approximately 7–12 minute intervals on the more popular routes, but careful attention should be paid to the route details listed for each section, since many routes operate only at certain times and on certain days of the week. Due to traffic congestion it has also been the practice in recent years to split routes and run them in sections, so that intending passengers should note carefully the details displayed on the vehicle destination board. Service intervals in other areas are usually longer. Some routes are served by one-man operated buses whereon passengers are required to pay the driver or obtain entry to the bus by passing an automatic ticket issuing machine.

All enquiries about services operated by London Buses may be made to the same locations as quoted for the Underground railways or at any London Bus Garage.

Other Bus Services

Green Line Coach services, not shown on the charts, operate across London and the green London Country buses operating into the outskirts of London, as listed in Section 5 at Uxbridge, for example, are controlled by London Country Bus Services Limited of Lesbourne Road, Reigate, Surrey, RH2 7LE. There is an office for personal or telephone enquiries at Victoria Coach Station, London, SW1 in respect of these services (Tel: 01-668 7261). Written enquiries should be addressed to the Public Relations Officer at Lesbourne Road, Reigate, Surrey (Tel: Reigate (0737) 42411).

Green Line and Nationwide express coach services are also operated by the National Bus Company from Victoria Coach Station, 164, Buckingham Palace Road, London, SW1 — opposite Eccleston Bridge. (Tel: 01-730 0202). Prior booking on such services is advisable, either at the Coach Station or at travel agents displaying the National Bus Company's sign, a mirrored italic 'N' designed to look like an arrow, usually in two colours, commonly red and blue.

London Taximeter Cabs

London taximeter cabs can be hired within the Metropolitan area, merely by signalling the driver of a free cab (indicated by an orange indicator sign above the windscreen reading 'TAXI' or 'FOR HIRE'). The fare is calculated from a combination of time hired and distance covered. Extras are charged for such items as additional luggage, passengers in excess of one and for hire between certain times in the night. Taxis may also be summoned or booked in advance by telephone from recognised cab-ranks which are listed in telephone directories under 'Taxi-Cab'.

Radio controlled cabs can be summoned by telephoning any of the following for journeys in the Metropolitan area:

01-286 4848	01-272 0272
01-253 5000	01-735 2000
01-286 0286	01-735 7770
01-286 6010	01-286 1125

USING THE TELEPHONE IN LONDON
Throughout this guide all telephone numbers have been given with the STD code prefix '01' which should only be dialled from telephones outside the London Area. All inter-exchange calls within the London Area may be made merely by dialling the last seven digits of the number, omitting the '01'. To obtain calls to exchanges outside the London Area, the number should be dialled, preceded by the relevant exchange code. These codes are displayed in telephone boxes and also in handbooks issued with the London Telephone directories which are available at post offices, libraries and in most call-boxes.

SANITARY DISPOSAL
Boatyards and other service points displaying the sign shown here are equipped to empty and recharge the new type of chemical toilet (with holding tank and flushing action).

A charge is normally made for this service.

Yards offering this service are listed in the Chart Directories.

King's Reach - Tug and barges after a barge driving match

Part I
London's River
The Tideway from Teddington to
Margaret Ness (Tripcock Point)

River Thames –
Teddington Lock to Margaret Ness (Tripcock Point)

Distance   29¾ statute land miles
Number of locks 1 (Richmond Half-tide Lock)
Tunnels   None
Bridges   29 (including Teddington Footbridge)
Branches   Brentford Creek, River Crane, River Wandle, Chelsea Creek, Grosvenor Canal, Deptford Creek, Bow Creek.

Maximum dimensions of craft (according to tide):
Headroom   12'6" (Hammersmith Bridge at HWS)
Length   Unlimited unless using Richmond Lock (250'0")
Beam   60'0" unless using Richmond Lock (26'8")
Draught   2'3" (Chiswick Bridge at LWS)
               13'6" (Richmond Railway Bridge at HWS)

Waterway Authority (for navigation)
The Port of London Authority
    Europe House, World Trade Centre, St Katharine's Way, London, E1 9AA (01-481 8484)

Director of Port Services and Harbour Master
    Thames House, St Andrews Road, Tilbury, Essex RM18 7JH (Tilbury (03752) 3444)

Thames Navigation Service
    Assistant Harbour Master (Upper Section)
    (Sections 1, 2, 3, and 4 of this guide)
    Tower Pier (Upper), London, EC3N 4PL
    (01-481 0720)

    Assistant Harbour Master (Lower Section)
    (Part IV of this guide)
    TNS Building, Royal Terrace Pier Road, Gravesend, Kent, DA12 2BG (Gravesend (0474) 67684)

Licensing   A licence to navigate the tidal Thames is not required.

PLA, TWA and privately leased piers' telephone numbers are quoted in the directory sections following each chart.

General enquiries concerning the TWA piers and the Thames Barrier should be referred to:
    The Operations Manager, Tideway Group, Thames Water Authority, Thorney House, 34, Smith Square, London, SW1P 3HF (01-222 6216)

PRACTICAL NAVIGATION
(based on notes supplied by the Port of London Authority)

The following notes are intended as a general guide to navigation on the first four sections of this guide. Full details are given in the PLA River Bye-Laws and International Regulations for Preventing Collisions at Sea.

1. Commercial Traffic
It is the normal practice to keep clear of all commercial traffic, as many of these types of craft have difficulty in manoeuvring and stopping. Barges towed by tugs are particularly difficult to manoeuvre through bridges, and many passenger service vessels can only alter course slowly. A careful look-out should be maintained astern as well as ahead, and appropriate avoiding action should always be taken in plenty of time.

2. Large Vessels
Remember that a large vessel under way is frequently confined to the deep water part of the channel. She cannot take quick avoiding action, and in narrow channels may not be able to take any avoiding action at all. Should any craft be in close proximity to a large vessel, a strong sense of self-preservation is recommended. Get clear as quickly as possible.

3. Right of Way
A vessel approaching any bridge or bend in the river when going against the tide should give way to a vessel approaching with the tide. This is particularly important near low water, when rowing eights going with the stream must go through Hammersmith Bridge, or the centre arch of Chiswick Bridge as it is too shallow elsewhere to be safe.

4. Overtaking
A vessel which is overtaking must keep clear of the slower vessel. Sound signals to indicate avoiding action should be made in good time. See note 10, below.

5. Crossing the River
When it becomes necessary to cross the river this should be done in the quickest manner practicable, with a sharp look-out for commercial traffic. Obviously any attempt to cross ahead of oncoming traffic in a strong tideway could prove very hazardous. A vessel crossing the river has no right of way over a vessel proceeding up or down.

6. Keep to the Right
When proceeding up or down river, all power driven vessels should, while it is safe and practicable, keep to the starboard (right hand) side of mid-channel.

7. Speed

Above Wandsworth there is a speed limit of 8 knots (9 mph) through the water. Below Wandsworth there is no specific limit, but speeds should be adjusted to ensure that there is no damage to persons or property caused by excessive wash. The speed 'limit' will therefore vary from craft to craft, but it should be remembered that speeding likely to cause damage in this way is an offence, making the owner or master of the craft liable to prosecution. The penalty is a fine of up to £1,000. Masters are advised that damage may be caused by speeds in excess of 10 knots, anywhere in the area covered by this guide.

8. Silencers

Attention is drawn to the necessity of fitting engines with efficient silencers.

9. Water Ski-ing

Water ski-ing or aquaplaning is entirely prohibited on the Thames Tideway within 200 yards of any public beach, bathing place, or residential property. If and where such restrictions do not apply then it is imperative that the towing boat has at least a crew of two – one to watch the boat and the other to watch the skier.

Sailing

The tidal Thames is extremely hazardous for small sailing vessels operated by persons with minimal local knowledge. It is *recommended* that sailboard sailing is restricted to the following areas:

    (a)   Westward (upstream) of Putney Bridge.

    (b)   Areas clear of both the navigation channel and approaches to commercial wharves in the following districts; Erith Rands, The Mucking Flats, Blyth Sands and All Hallows, and Southend Pier to Canvey Island, Thorney Bay.

10. Sound Signals

These signals are made by power driven vessels to indicate their own intended actions to other vessels. Apart from the first four of the following signals, which are internationally recognised, these signals only apply on the Thames.

	MEANING	SIGNAL
1.	I am altering my course to **Starboard**	**One** short blast
2.	I am altering my course to **Port**	**Two** short blasts
3.	My engines are going **Astern**	**Three** short blasts
4.	I do not consider you are taking sufficient action to **Keep Clear** of me	**Five** or more short and rapid blasts
5.	I am **Turning** round with my head swinging to **Starboard**	**Four** short blasts followed by **One** short blast
6.	I am **Turning** round with my head swinging to **Port**	**Four** short blasts followed by **Two** short blasts

7. I am about to **Get Underway** i.e. depart from moorings, jetty or dock entrance	**One** prolonged blast
8. I am about to **Overtake** on your **Starboard** side	**Two** long blasts followed by **One** short blast
9. I am about to **Overtake** on your **Port** side	**Two** long blasts followed by **Two** short blasts
10. You may **Overtake** me	**One** long blast followed by **One** short blast followed by **One** long blast and **One** short blast in that order

WRECKS AND OBSTRUCTIONS

The use of green is discontinued as a colour specifically for wreck buoys. 'New Dangers' (i.e. a newly discovered hazard not yet shown on charts or promulgated by Notice to Mariners, and thus including wrecks) are marked by one or more cardinal or lateral buoys in accordance with IALA rules. If a light is used it will be Quick Flashing (Q) or Very Quick Flashing (VQ): if cardinal it will be a white light, if lateral a red or green light.

A vessel engaged in underwater work will exhibit by day three shapes in a vertical line, the highest and lowest being red balls and the middle one a white diamond. By night three lights are shown in the same colours. The nature of the work performed by these craft usually necessitates breast wires extending outwards from the sides of the vessel and they should therefore be given a wide berth. The side of the vessel on which an obstruction exists should be indicated by two all-round red lights or two balls in a vertical line. The side on which other vessels may safely pass is indicated by two all-round green lights or two diamond shapes in a vertical line.

A red flag,* or under new regulations agreed — a white and blue flag with a swallowtail (International Code flag A) — means that divers are down. Keep well clear and go slowly to avoid making any wash which might endanger them. At night, a red flashing light is displayed.

Obstructions which are not completely covered by water are marked by a post carrying two red balls, or red lights at night, placed horizontally. Such marks to be left to starboard when proceeding with the flood may show two green shapes or lights.

BRIDGES

Unobstructed arches for navigation are denoted by two orange/red lights placed horizontally at the head of the open span. Other spans may be clear, as shown in the tables which follow.

A triangle of three red discs or three red lights hanging apex downwards from the arch of a bridge indicates that the arch is closed to navigation.†

*Notwithstanding the new agreement to fly International Code Flag 'A', the PLA Bye-laws state that a red flag shall be shown at the position as close as possible to the divers' point of entry to the water.

†If the span of a bridge is restricted in headroom, due to maintenance or repair work, a wisp of straw will be displayed on the underside of the scaffolding or other works on the span. At night, the wisp of straw will be replaced by a WHITE light.

SUNKEN CRAFT – OWNER'S LIABILITY

Should any craft be unfortunate enough to sink in or near the shipping channel, the PLA have, under statutory powers, the right to remove the wreck by means of salvage craft. All expenses are recoverable from the owner of the craft at the time of sinking.

If a vessel in trying to avoid another runs aground or into a jetty, the owner of the craft may find himself sued for heavy damages.

Owners are strongly recommended to take insurance cover against these possibilities and are reminded that when a boat is loaned the owner is still legally responsible, whether he is on board or not.

There is a responsibility on the part of the owner or master of a vessel to report any accident involving casualty, sinking, fire, explosion or damage to the property of a third party to the nearest Assistant Harbour Master's Office or to the Assistant Harbour Master in person or one of his officers as soon as possible following such an accident.

WIDTHS OF SPANS AND HEADWAYS OF TIDEWAY BRIDGES

All headway dimensions are given from MHWS shown in line 'H'.
Span widths are given at MHWS shown in line 'S'.
Navigation arches are indicated by heavy rule round the relevant dimensions.
Where no headway is quoted the arch is unnavigable.
In some cases the end spans are obstructed by quays, piers or embankments and should be avoided unless shown in heavy rule.

Name of Bridge		Middlesex Bank			DOWNSTREAM			Surrey Bank
Richmond Road	H		11'9"	13'3"	17'6"	14'0"	11'9"	
	S		45'0"	50'0"	60'0"	50'0"	45'0"	
Richmond Rail	H			18'0"	17'6"	17'9"		
	S			100'0"	100'0"	100'0"		
Twickenham Road	H			19'0"	19'6"	19'0"		
	S			97'0"	102'0"	97'0"		
Richmond Foot	H		Boat Rollers	18'3"	18'3"	18'3"	Lock	See note on p. 25
	S			66'0"	66'0"	66'0"		
Kew Road	H			14'9"	17'6"	14'9"		
	S			116'0"	133'0"	116'0"		
Kew Rail	H		18'0"	18'0"	17'9"	18'3"	18'3"	
	S		103'0"	103'0"	103'0"	103'0"	103'0"	
Chiswick Road	H			22'3"	22'9"	22'3"		
	S			125'0"	150'0"	125'0"		
Barnes Rail	H			18'0"	17'9"	18'0"		
	S			120'0"	120'0"	120'0"		
Hammersmith Road	H			—	12'6"	—		
	S			143'0"	400'0"	145'0"		
Putney Road	H		12'6"	15'9"	18'3"	15'9"	12'6"	
	S		112'0"	129'0"	144'0"	129'0"	112'0"	
Fulham Railway	H	Over Shore	20'9"	21'9"	22'6"	24'0"	25'0"	Over Shore
	S		143'0"	143'0"	143'0"	143'0"	143'0"	
Wandsworth Road	H			9'6"	19'0"	9'6"		
	S			164'0"	283'0"	164'0"		
Battersea Rail	H		20'9"	20'6"	20'6"	20'9"	20'9"	
	S		137'0"	137'0"	137'0"	137'0"	137'0"	
Battersea Road	H		9'3"	13'9"	18'3"	13'9"	9'3"	
	S		113'0"	140'0"	163'0"	140'0"	113'0"	
Albert Road	H		—	16'0"	16'0"	—		
	S		145'0"	182'0"	182'0"	149'0"		
Chelsea Road	H			—	22'0"	—		
	S			163'0"	332'0"	163'0"		
Victoria Rail	H		20'6"	20'0"	20'0"	20'3"		
	S		174'0"	174'0"	174'0"	174'0"		
Vauxhall Road	H		13'9"	17'9"	18'6"	17'9"	13'9"	
	S		130'0"	144'0"	149'0"	144'0"	130'0"	
Lambeth Road	H		11'6"	17'6"	21'3"	17'6"	11'6"	
	S		125'0"	149'0"	165'0"	149'0"	125'0"	

Name of Bridge								
Westminster Road	H	14'6"	16'3"	17'9"	18'0"	17'9"	16'3"	14'6"
	S	94'0"	104'0"	114'0"	119'0"	114'0"	104'0"	94'0"
Charing Cross & Hungerford	H	23'0"	23'0"	23'0"	23'3"	23'6"	24'5"	
	S	152'0"	153'0"	153'0"	151'0"	152'0"	152'0"	
Waterloo Road	H		–	28'3"	28'3"	28'3"	–	
	S		231'0"	238'0"	238'0"	238'0"	231'0"	
Blackfriars Road	H		–	19'6"	23'3"	19'9"	–	
	S		154'0"	173'0"	185'0"	173'0"	154'0"	
Blackfriars Rail	H		–	23'3"	23'0"	23'3"	23'3"	
	S		–	175'0"	186'0"	175'0"	180'0"	
Southwark Road	H		–	21'6"	24'3"	21'6"	–	
	S		123'0"	131'0"	140'0"	131'0"	123'0"	
Cannon St Rail	H		21'3"	23'6"	23'3"	23'6"	24'0"	
	S		123'0"	134'0"	135'0"	135'0"	125'0"	
London Bridge Road	H			24'9"	29'3"	24'9"		
	S			259'0"	326'0"	170'0"		
Tower Bridge Road (shut)	H			28'6"	28'6"	28'6"		
	S			270'0"	200'0"	270'0"		
Tower Bridge Road (open)	H			28'6"	139'6"	28'6"		
	S			270'0"	200'0"	270'0"		

Name of Bridge		Surrey Bank		UPSTREAM			Middlesex Bank	
Tower Bridge Road (open)	H			28'6"	139'6"	28'6"		
	S			270'0"	200'0"	270'0"		
Tower Bridge Road (shut)	H			28'6"	28'6"	28'6"		
	S			270'0"	200'0"	270'0"		
London Bridge Road	H			24'9"	29'3"	24'9"		
	S			170'0"	326'0"	259'0"		
Cannon Street Rail	H		24'0"	23'6"	23'3"	23'6"	21'3"	
	S		125'0"	135'0"	135'0"	134'0"	123'0"	
Southwark Road	H		–	21'6"	24'3"	21'6"	–	
	S		123'0"	131'0"	140'0"	131'0"	123'0"	
Blackfriars Rail	H		23'3"	23'3"	23'0"	23'3"	–	
	S		180'0"	175'0"	186'0"	175'0"	–	
Blackfriars Road	H			19'9"	23'3"	19'6"	–	
	S		154'0"	173'0"	185'0"	173'0"	154'0"	
Waterloo Road	H			28'3"	28'3"	28'3"		
	S		231'0"	238'0"	238'0"	238'0"	231'0"	
Charing Cross & Hungerford	H	24'5"	23'6"	23'3"	23'0"	23'0"	23'0"	
	S	152'0"	152'0"	151'0"	153'0"	153'0"	152'0"	
Westminster Road	H	14'6"	16'3"	17'9"	18'0"	17'9"	16'3"	14'6"
	S	94'0"	104'0"	114'0"	119'0"	114'0"	104'0"	94'0"
Lambeth Road	H		11'6"	17'6"	18'6"	17'6"	11'6"	
	S		125'0"	149'0"	165'0"	149'0"	125'0"	
Vauxhall Road	H		13'9"	17'9"	18'6"	17'9"	13'9"	
	S		130'0"	144'0"	149'0"	144'0"	130'0"	
Victoria Rail	H		20'3"	20'0"	20'0"	20'6"		
	S		174'0"	174'0"	174'0"	174'0"		
Chelsea Road	H			–	22'0"	–		
	S			163'0"	332'0"	163'0"		

17

Bridge		Note	C1	C2	C3	C4	C5	Note
Albert Road	H		−	16'0"	16'0"	−		
	S		149'0"	182'0"	182'0"	145'0"		
Battersea Road	H		9'3"	13'9"	18'3"	13'9"	9'3"	
	S		113'0"	140'0"	163'0"	140'0"	113'0"	
Battersea Rail	H		20'9"	20'9"	20'6"	20'6"	20'9"	
	S		137'0"	137'0"	137'0"	137'0"	137'0"	
Wandsworth Road	H			9'6"	19'0"	9'6"		
	S			164'0"	283'0"	164'0"		
Fulham Rail	H	Over Shore	25'0"	24'0"	22'6"	21'9"	20'9"	Over Shore
	S		143'0"	143'0"	143'0"	143'0"	143'0"	
Putney Road	H		12'6"	15'9"	18'3"	15'9"	12'6"	
	S		112'0"	129'0"	144'0"	129'0"	112'0"	
Hammersmith Road	H			−	12'6"	−		
	S			145'0"	400'0"	143'0"		
Barnes Rail	H			18'0"	17'9"	18'0"		
	S			120'0"	120'0"	120'0"		
Chiswick Road	H			22'3"	22'9"	22'3"		
	S			125'0"	150'0"	125'0"		
Kew Rail	H		18'3"	18'3"	17'9"	18'0"	18'0"	
	S		103'0"	103'0"	103'0"	103'0"	103'0"	
Kew Road	H			14'9"	17'6"	14'9"		
	S			116'0"	133'0"	116'0"		
Richmond Foot	H	Lock		18'3"	18'3"	18'3"		Boat Rollers See note on p. 25
	S			66'0"	66'0"	66'0"		
Twickenham Road	H			19'0"	19'6"	19'0"		
	S			97'0"	102'0"	97'0"		
Richmond Rail	H			17'9"	17'6"	18'0"		
	S			100'0"	100'0"	100'0"		
Richmond Road	H		11'9"	14'0"	17'6"	13'3"	11'9"	
	S		45'0"	50'0"	60'0"	50'0"	45'0"	

HEADWAYS AND DEPTHS OF CENTRE SPANS OF TIDEWAY BRIDGES

HOW TO USE THE TABLES

In the 'Headways and Depths of Centre Spans of Tideway Bridges' table all measurements are related to Chart Datum, which represents the height of the Lowest Astronomical Tide (LAT). To find the depth of water at Low Water Springs for any bridge you therefore take the figure given as the depth in centre span *below* Chart Datum and add the figure (if any) shown under MLWS (Mean Low Water Springs). At the same time to find the air draught, headroom, or mast clearance of the same bridge, you *deduct* the MLWS figure from the 'Headway of Centre Span above: Chart Datum' figure in the first column of the table. The other columns of the table give quick references to the other states of the tide and the air draughts for MHWS are quoted readily worked out in Column 2.

Most tide tables give times in GMT (Greenwich Mean Time). No allowance is usually made for the operation of British Summer Time (BST). During British Summer Time (from late March to late October) ONE hour should be ADDED to the tide times shown in the tables.

HEADWAYS AND DEPTHS OF CENTRE SPANS OF TIDEWAY BRIDGES (Imperial)

Name of Bridge	Type	Headway of Centre Span above:		Depth in Centre Span below Chart Datum	Tidal Levels above Chart Datum				Distance above London Bridge in Land miles	Chart No.
		Chart Datum	MHWS		MHWS	MLWS	MHWN	MLWN		
Richmond Road	Arch	26'0"	17'6"	5'9"	8'6"	—	4'6"	—	16.1	3
Richmond Rail	Arch	26'0"	17'6"	5'0"	8'6"	—	4'6"	—	15.7	3
Twickenham Rd	Arch	28'0"	19'6"	6'3"	8'6"	—	4'6"	—	15.7	3
Richmond Foot	Arch	34'3"	18'3"	2'3"	16'0"	*	12'0"	*	15.5	3
Kew Road	Arch	35'0"	17'6"	4'0"	17'6"	—	13'3"	0'3"	13.0	5
Kew Railway	Flat	35'9"	18'3"	3'3"	17'6"	—	13'9"	0'3"	12.6	5
Chiswick Road	Arch	40'3"	22'9"	2'3"	17'6"	—	13'9"	0'3"	11.8	6
Barnes Rail	Arch	36'0"	17'9"	3'0"	18'3"	—	14'0"	0'9"	11.0	6
Hammersmith Rd	Susp	31'0"	12'6"	4'0"	18'6"	—	15'0"	1'0"	9.2	7
Putney Road	Arch	37'6"	18'3"	4'3"	19'6"	0'3"	15'9"	1'3"	7.4	8
Fulham Rail	Flat	42'0"	22'6"	4'3"	19'6"	0'3"	15'9"	1'3"	7.3	8
Wandsworth Rd	Arch	39'0"	19'0"	5'3"	20'0"	0'3"	16'0"	1'9"	6.3	9
Battersea Rail	Arch	40'6"	20'6"	4'0"	20'0"	0'3"	16'0"	1'9"	5.6	10
Battersea Road	Arch	38'6"	18'3"	5'0"	20'3"	0'3"	16'6"	2'0"	4.9	10
Albert Road	Susp	36'3"	16'0"	5'0"	20'3"	0'3"	16'9"	2'0"	4.7	10
Chelsea Road	Susp	42'6"	22'0"	6'9"	20'6"	0'9"	17'3"	2'3"	3.9	11
Victoria Rail	Susp	40'6"	20'0"	5'0"	20'6"	0'9"	17'3"	2'3"	3.8	11
Vauxhall Road	Arch	40'0"	18'6"	4'0"	21'6"	0'9"	17'6"	2'6"	2.9	11
Lambeth Road	Arch	43'3"	21'3"	5'6"	22'0"	1'0"	18'3"	3'0"	2.4	12
Westminster Rd	Arch	40'3"	18'0"	2'6"	22'3"	1'3"	18'6"	3'6"	1.9	12
Charing Cross Railway & Hungerford Foot	Flat	45'3"	23'0"	5'3"	22'3"	1'3"	18'6"	3'6"	1.5	12
Waterloo Road	Arch	50'6"	28'3"	4'0"	22'3"	1'3"	18'6"	3'6"	1.3	12
Blackfriars Rd	Arch	46'0"	23'3"	5'9"	22'9"	1'3"	19'0"	4'0"	0.7	13
Blackfriars Rail	Arch	45'6"	23'0"	5'9"	22'9"	1'3"	19'0"	4'0"	0.7	13
Southwark Road	Arch	47'0"	24'3"	8'3"	22'9"	1'3"	19'0"	4'0"	0.3	13
Cannon St Rail	Flat	46'0"	23'3"	7'6"	22'9"	1'3"	19'0"	4'0"	0.2	13
London Road	Arch	52'6"	29'3"	3'6"	23'3"	1'9"	19'6"	4'3"	0.0	13
Tower Road (shut)	Basc	51'9"	28'6"	3'6" }	23'3"	1'3"	19'6"	4'3"	0.6 below	14
(open)	Basc	162'9"	139'6"	17'3" }						

*Richmond Footbridge centre three spans are closed at Low Water. Passage only available via Richmond Lock under span on Surrey Bank or boat rollers under span on Middlesex Bank. See note on p. 25.

HEADWAYS AND DEPTHS OF CENTRE SPANS OF TIDEWAY BRIDGES (Metric)
(Shown in metres to 1 decimal place)

Name of Bridge	Type	Headway of Centre Span above:		Depth in Centre Span below Chart Datum	Tidal Levels above Chart Datum				Distance above London Bridge in Kilometres	Chart No.
		Chart Datum	MHWS		MHWS	MLWS	MHWN	MLWN		
Richmond Road	Arch	7.9	5.3	1.7	2.6	—	1.4	—	25.6	3
Richmond Rail	Arch	7.9	5.3	1.5	2.6	—	1.4	—	24.8	3
Twickenham Rd	Arch	8.5	5.9	1.9	2.6	—	1.4	—	24.8	3
Richmond Foot	Arch	10.4	5.5	0.7	4.9	*	3.7	*	24.5	3
Kew Road	Arch	10.6	5.3	1.2	5.3	—	4.1	0.1	20.7	5
Kew Railway	Flat	10.9	5.6	1.0	5.3	—	4.2	0.1	20.0	5
Chiswick	Arch	12.2	6.9	0.7	5.3	—	4.2	0.1	18.7	6
Barnes Rail	Arch	10.9	5.4	0.9	5.5	—	4.3	0.2	17.4	6
Hammersmith Rd	Susp	9.4	3.7	1.2	5.7	—	4.6	0.3	14.6	7
Putney Road	Arch	11.4	5.5	1.3	5.9	0.1	4.8	0.4	11.7	8
Fulham Rail	Flat	12.8	6.9	1.3	5.9	0.1	4.8	0.4	11.5	8
Wandsworth Rd	Arch	11.9	5.8	1.6	6.1	0.1	4.9	0.5	9.9	9
Battersea Rail	Arch	12.2	6.1	1.2	6.1	0.1	4.9	0.5	8.8	10
Battersea Road	Arch	11.7	5.5	1.5	6.2	0.1	5.0	0.6	7.6	10
Albert Road	Susp	11.1	4.9	1.5	6.2	0.1	5.1	0.6	7.3	10
Chelsea Road	Susp	12.9	6.6	2.1	6.3	0.2	5.2	0.7	6.1	11
Victoria Rail	Arch	12.3	6.0	1.5	6.3	0.2	5.2	0.7	5.9	11
Vauxhall Road	Arch	12.1	5.6	1.2	6.5	0.2	5.3	0.8	4.5	11
Lambeth Road	Arch	13.1	6.5	1.7	6.6	0.3	5.5	0.9	3.8	12
Westminster Rd	Arch	12.2	5.4	0.8	6.8	0.4	5.6	1.1	3.0	12
Charing Cross Railway & Hungerford Foot	Flat	13.8	7.0	1.6	6.8	0.4	5.6	1.1	2.4	12
Waterloo Road	Arch	15.3	8.5	1.2	6.8	0.4	5.6	1.1	2.1	12
Blackfriars Rd	Arch	14.0	7.1	1.7	6.9	0.4	5.8	1.2	1.0	13
Blackfriars Rail	Arch	13.9	7.0	1.7	6.9	0.4	5.8	1.2	1.0	13
Southwark Road	Arch	14.3	7.4	2.5	6.9	0.4	5.8	1.2	0.4	13
Cannon St Rail	Flat	14.0	7.1	2.3	6.9	0.4	5.8	1.2	0.3	13
London Bridge	Arch	16.0	8.9	1.1	7.1	0.5	5.9	1.3	0.0	13
Tower Bridge (shut)	Basc	15.7	8.6	5.2	7.1	0.4	5.9	1.3	1.0 below	14
(open)		49.6	42.5	5.2	7.1	0.4	5.9	1.3		

*Richmond Footbridge centre three spans are closed at Low Water. Passage only available via Richmond Lock under span on Surrey Bank or boat rollers under span on Middlesex Bank. See note on p. 25.

KEY TO THAMES CHARTS (1 – 20)

Tidal constants read in descending order in the panel:

High Water (Springs)
Low Water (Springs)   Hours and minutes
High Water (Neaps)
Low Water (Neaps)

A + sign in front of the figure indicates time after HW or LW London Bridge
A – sign in front of the figure indicates time before HW or LW London Bridge

Times are given in hours and minutes, but are *approximate* only, having been obtained from a number of different authorities and from personal observation at various points along the river.

Readings relate to the nearest bridge, tide-lock or dock entrance shown on the chart.

andard Scale of all Charts

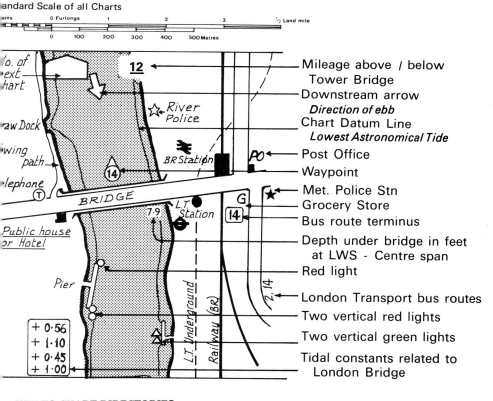

KEY TO CHART DIRECTORIES

A = Angler's supplies	G = Butane gas supplier	R = Repairs
B = Boatbuilders	H = Boat hirer	S = Sanitary station
C = Chandlers	I = Insurance	T = Telephone
D = Diesel fuel	L = Landing stage	U = Refuse disposal
E = Marine engineers	M = Moorings	W = Water point
F = Ferry or trip boats	P = Petrol fuel	

W. Hammerton & Co. Ltd
Marble Hill Boathouse, Twickenham, Middx
(01-892 9620)

Ferry Operators and Self-Drive Hire, Moorings
(F, H, M)

Thames Information Centre
Gresham House, Twickenham Road, Feltham,
Middx (01-894 5511)

River information in general

Richmond Yacht Club
Eel Pie Island (01-892 9679)

Cruising Club (ATYC)

Twickenham Yacht Club
Riverside, Twickenham (01-892 8487)

Cruising Club (ATYC)

Twickenham Rowing Club
Eel Pie Island (01-892 5291)

Rowing Club

Draw Docks
Twickenham Draw Dock, Twickenham Embankment, Church Road
White Swan Inn Draw Dock, Riverside, Twickenham
Ham Landing, Ham Fields
Petersham Draw Dock, Petersham Meadow, via River Lane

Towing Path
Surrey Bank downstream as far as River Lane.
Middlesex Bank downstream from Orleans Road to Petersham Ferry (Chart No. 3).

Working Ferries
Twickenham
Hammerton's

The Barmy Arms *(Inn),* The Embankment, Twickenham (01-892 0863)
The Eel Pie *(Inn),* 9, Church Street, Twickenham (01-891 1717)
The White Swan *(Inn),* Riverside, Twickenham (01-892 2166)
(A) E. Thurston, 360, Richmond Road, Twickenham (01-892 4175) *Fishing tackle*

Weir Sluice being raised alongside Richmond Lock

Section 1 **Teddington to Kew**

THERE IS A SPEED LIMIT OF 8 KNOTS (9 mph) THROUGHOUT THIS SECTION

Virtually devoid of commercial traffic, apart from the odd dredger or ballast lighter, the Thames below Teddington is still quiet and unspoilt with little hint of the urbanised surroundings which follow in the next section. Teddington Lock is not the point of no return that many imagine it to be, merely because the fleets of hire cruisers let on the Upper Thames are prohibited from venturing below the lock. Navigation to Richmond is perfectly possible on all states of the tide, due to the installation in 1894 of the tidal barrier and lock at Richmond, which always operate to maintain a navigable depth of at least 5'9" between Teddington and Richmond. Below Richmond, the river winds past Isleworth, Old Deer Park, Kew Gardens and Syon Park, before meeting any lighter traffic which might be bound for Brentford on the Grand Union Canal.

In Syon Reach, there are numerous shoals on the Surrey side of the channel. Craft drawing more than 2'6" are therefore advised not to navigate this reach around low water. At Kew Bridge, the centre span should be navigated, since there are often passenger launches berthing at or leaving Kew Gardens Pier, which is under the Surrey arch. All information regarding tides, and moorings available administered by the Port of London Authority in this area are available from the Richmond Lock Office (Tel: 01-940 0634).

The charts for this section end just below Kew Railway Bridge, which is partially obstructed by Oliver's Ait, which is on the upstream side of the bridge. The navigation channel lies on the Surrey side of the ait.

This section may be approached from the Upper Thames by way of Teddington Lock which is controlled by the Thames Water Authority. Craft requiring to enter the Upper Thames *from* the section must be registered with the Authority beforehand. Owners are required to pay an annual or triennial fee for registration, when a registration certificate and licence plate will be issued. Payment of the fee *includes* lock tolls. Craft so registered are subject to inspection by the Authority's officers to ensure that they conform to certain specifications with regard to engine, fuel, gas and sanitary installations. Copies of the Bye-Laws and the Specifications are obtainable from the Head Office of the Authority at Nugent House, Vastern Road, Reading, Berks (Tel: Reading (0734) 593333).

If intending to continue your cruise from the Thames into the River Wey at Shepperton, your cruiser will also have to be licensed with the navigation authority for the River Wey, the National Trust. The address to write to is: The Manager, Wey and Godalming Navigation, National Trust, Dapdune Wharf, Woodbridge Road, Guildford, Surrey (Tel: Guildford (0483) 61389).

Both authorities issue short-period licences for visiting craft.

Craft using the tideway below Teddington do not need to be licensed by the PLA. If entering the canal system, however, at Brentford, Limehouse Basin or Bow Creek a British Waterways Board craft licence will be required. Details of such licences and the fees are obtainable from: The Craft Licensing Supervisor, British Waterways Board, Willow Grange, Church Road, Watford, Herts WD1 3QA (Tel: Watford (0923) 26422).

Teddington Lock is controlled by the Thames Water Authority and is manned by keepers 24 hours a day, throughout the year. Passage of the lock is not affected by the tides below it, since the sluices at Richmond maintain a depth between high and 'half' tide on all tides, about 5'9" above theoretical Lowest Astronomical Tide.

Teddington Locks	(Tel: 01-940 8723)
New (Barge) Lock	650'0" long 24'9" wide 8'7" maximum draught
Old (Launch) Lock	177'11" long 24'4" wide 9'2" maximum draught
Skiff Lock	49'6" long 5'10" wide 3'7" maximum draught

Maximum fall of all three locks (according to tide) 8'10". (Minimum Low Water Springs).

Upstream Approach to Teddington Lock

Teddington lock signal lights. — Lighted signals are placed at the lower end of Teddington barge lock to direct traffic proceeding upstream through Teddington Locks:

The signal lights indicate as follows:

(i) Central red lights.	Barge and launch locks not ready for upstream traffic.
(ii) Flashing red arrow pointing left.	Barge lock not ready for upstream traffic. When lock is available the red arrow is replaced by a flashing white arrow.
(iii) Flashing red arrow pointing right.	Launch lock not ready for upstream traffic. When lock is available the red arrow is replaced by a flashing white arrow.

Vessels using the small skiff lock are not subject to the above signals, and should proceed direct to the tail of this lock and await the directions of the lock staff.

Do not enter the Barge Lock just because you see that it is open. The Old (Launch) Lock is more suitable for smaller private craft (*see dimensions given above*), but is out of sight from the main channel to the right of the lock island on which the signals are placed. A lay-by for mooring, to await lock opening is provided on the island between the signals and the launch lock.

TIDES

The River Thames is fully tidal as far upstream as Richmond Footbridge. High Tide at Brentford, 1½ miles below Richmond Footbridge, occurs approximately 1 hour *after* High Tide at London Bridge. High Tide reaches Richmond Footbridge about 6 minutes *later*. During periods of neap tides, High Tide may occur up to 10 minutes earlier at each point. *See the Tidal Constant panels on the charts.*

Between Teddington and Richmond Footbridge, to maintain an adequate depth of water for navigation the river is kept above half-tide level by means of vertical overhead sluices suspended from Richmond Footbridge. When raised — from approximately 2 hours before High Water to 2 hours after High Water — passage through the central three arches is possible, denoted by two fixed orange lights at the head of each span.

If the sluices are lowered, preventing passage, the orange lights are replaced by three red discs in triangular formation apex down below each span by day, or red fixed lights in the same formation at night, and craft *must* use Richmond Lock, which is located beneath the end span of the bridge on the Surrey Bank.

A toll for use of the lock is payable to the keeper at the time of passage. Passage through the footbridge, when open, is free.

Richmond Lock is controlled by the Port of London Authority and is manned 24 hours a day, daily. Passage below the lock, by craft drawing more than 2'6" should not be attempted at low tide owing to shoals in Syon Reach and reaches in later Sections, further downstream.

> *Richmond Lock* (Tel: 01-940 0643)
> 250'0" long 26'8" wide.
> Maximum fall (according to tide) 10'0"

Skiffs and canoes may use the boat rollers located below the last arch of the footbridge against the Middlesex Bank.

GRAND UNION CANAL (MAIN LINE)

Entry to the Grand Union Canal is made by entering Brentford Creek on the Middlesex Bank about 1½ miles below Richmond Lock and Footbridge. From upstream the entrance is inconspicuous but lies just below Syon Park against which there are numerous barge moorings.

Thames Lock (No 101) is the first lock and is paired, and is worked on weekdays, except Bank Holidays, from two hours before High Water in Brentford Creek until two hours after, within the period 0600–2200. If the times of High Water are more than one hour outside this period so that the working period would be less than one hour NO working will take place and the lock will remain closed.

Brentford Lock (No 100) is the next lock and is only part tidal, being open on weekdays all day from 0700 hours to 1800 hours. On Saturdays and Sundays and on certain summer Bank Holidays within the period 0600 to 2200 both locks are worked from two hours before High Water to two hours after, only. If the times of High Water are more than one hour outside this period NO working will take place as explained above. However if passage is essential or required in an emergency you should telephone the duty keeper at Thames Lock on 01-568 2779 during that lock's working hours. Working of these locks by boat crews is prohibited.

All locks are designed to pass craft of maximum dimensions 72′0″ long 14′3″ wide, drawing 3′6″. The actual depth quoted by some authorities may exceed this figure but allowances have been made for silting.

If planning to enter or leave these locks, it is strongly recommended that skippers telephone the lock-keeper well in advance on 01-560 1120 or out of office hours on 01-560 8942 from Teddington, Southall or from the point of departure downstream on the River Thames.

On high tides (springs) you should note that the headroom of Dock Road Bridge which crosses the tail of Thames Locks which are tidal can be as little as 7′0″. You may therefore have to be prepared to wait outside the lock in the creek until the tide has fallen sufficiently for your vessel to clear the bridge. The spring tidal range at this point is approximately 17 feet. Since the pound above Thames Locks is part tidal the headroom under Brentford High Street Bridge (No. 209) may also be restricted.

TRANSFER PASSAGES BETWEEN TEDDINGTON AND BRENTFORD
Before attempting a passage in either direction, consult the current tide tables for the times of High Water at London Bridge. These figures are published annually by the Admiralty, and may also be found in Reed's Almanac and the PLA Tide Tables. Times of High Water at London Bridge are also published daily in a number of national newspapers in their meteorological information columns.

If applicable (March to October) ADD 1 hour to convert times given in Greenwich Mean Time to British Summer Time. Look up the times of High Water on the day you intend effecting the transfer and add the High Water Constant which is taken by the BWB lock-keepers at Brentford as 1 hour exactly irrespective of the slight variations shown in the Charts. To establish whether tides are approaching Springs or Neaps, as a rough guide, the Spring Tide maximum approaches up to 7.9 metres at London Bridge or about 26 feet. Neap Tides can be as low as a maximum of 5.5 metres or 18 feet. Figures in feet or metres are sometimes quoted in the national press as a guide. Accurate figures are given in the tables.

Now, within the normal working hours period shown above for Brentford and Thames Locks find out over what period they will be available. (Note that Teddington need not concern you as Teddington Locks do not cease operation at half-tide.)

Also bear in mind that to avoid working through Richmond Lock you will want to time your passage through Richmond at around High Water. Additionally you will have a more comfortable passage if you use the tide to assist you in either direction.

The best time to leave Teddington, therefore, is on the last of the incoming (flood) tide so that from slack water you will get the benefit of the ebb as you proceed downstream. The passage to Brentford should take about 1 to 1½ hours so that you will still have up to an hour to spare before Thames Lock is closed (provided you are not using a late afternoon tide which is going to bring you into Brentford Creek after the lock staff there have gone off duty!).

The best time to leave Brentford for Teddington is as soon as possible after the locks there open so that you will be carried upstream to Teddington on the flood. Do not be too eager, though, as you may find that you will arrive at Richmond Footbridge while the sluices are still down. Due to differences in levels caused by the amount of upland water coming from Teddington Weir it may be that the flood tide will have to rise higher than usual in order to make a level with the upper section.

On approaching Teddington take note of the signals at the tail of the lock island as to which of the locks you should use. *See previous notes and diagram.*

WORKING UPSTREAM TO BRENTFORD OR TEDDINGTON FROM LOWER THAMES

Obviously the method of calculating passages into the Grand Union Canal at Brentford from the Lower Thames is similar, but remember that you will probably wish to use the flood tide to assist your passage, and not the ebb as in the case of coming downstream from Teddington and Richmond.

If leaving London Bridge or, possibly, Limehouse Basin, you will wish to utilise as much of the flood tide as possible. If in the tideway at Low Tide, you may start your journey at slack water upstream, when you will have ample time to reach Brentford from as far down as Woolwich Ferry assuming a cruiser speed of about 3 to 4 knots.

Exit into the tideway from Limehouse Basin via the ship lock is possible about 3½ hours before high water at London Bridge, which will give you about 4½ hours of flood water which, again, is ample time to reach Brentford, possibly even Teddington. Remember, though that the tide will turn progressively earlier the shorter distance you travel upstream.

Again, it is advisable from the London area to telephone the lock-keeper at Brentford to arrange an estimated time of arrival with him and to obtain his advice concerning any variation of tide or the depth in relation to the headroom at Dock Road Bridge. (Tel: 01-560 1120).

If working to Teddington, there is no need to telephone as lock staff are always on the look-out for craft, except during meal breaks or overnight when it may be necessary to land and request their assistance. If intending passage at night it is courteous to advise Teddington lock-keeper of an estimated time of arrival. This will avoid any undue delay for you. (Tel: 01-940 8723).

Tidal Constants on London Bridge		Mean Tidal Ranges	
HWS + 1 hr 18m LWS * — HWN + 1 hr 08m LWN * —	at Teddington Lock	Springs Neaps	8'6" 2.56m 4'6" 1.37m

Duration of Rise and Fall of Average Spring and Neap Tides			
Flood		*Ebb*	
Springs	**Neaps**	**Springs**	**Neaps**
*2 hrs 00m	*2 hrs 00m	*2 hrs 00m	*2 hrs 00m

Ebb tide sets toward	
Reach	*Bank*
Teddington Reach	Middlesex
Cross Deep	Middlesex

*The sluices at Richmond Lock maintain this section above a tidal level of 5'9", termed *half-tide*. The tide therefore only rises and falls when the sluices are open. The tidal level therefore remains static for about 8 hrs 15 m over Low Water Springs and 8 hrs 45 m over Low Water Neaps.

CHART DIRECTORY
For key to letter references see p. 21

Thames Water Authority (Headquarters)
Nugent House, Vastern Road, Reading,
Berks. RG1 8DB (Reading (0734) 593333)

Navigation Authority for the Upper Thames

Thames Water
Navigation Inspector (No. 4 District)
Riverside Works, Fordbridge Road,
Sunbury-on-Thames (Sunbury (09327) 81946)

Navigation Inspector controlling section down to Boundary Stone

Teddington Locks (TWA)
(01-940 8723)

Lock-keeper's Office
Launch licences issued

Tough Brothers Limited
Teddington Wharf, Ferry Road, Teddington,
Middx (01-977 4494 or 01-943 3279)

Boatyard
(B, C, D, E, G, I, M, R, W)

Swan Island Harbour
Swan Island, 1, Strawberry Vale, Twickenham,
Middx (01-892 2861)

Boatyard and Moorings
(D, M, R, W, E, S, T)

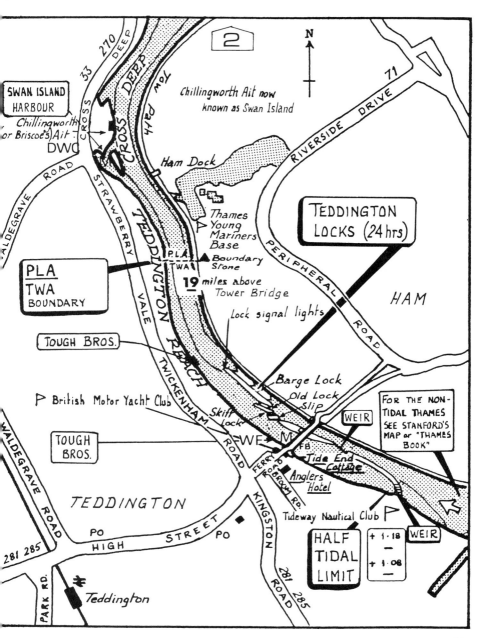

2 Twickenham

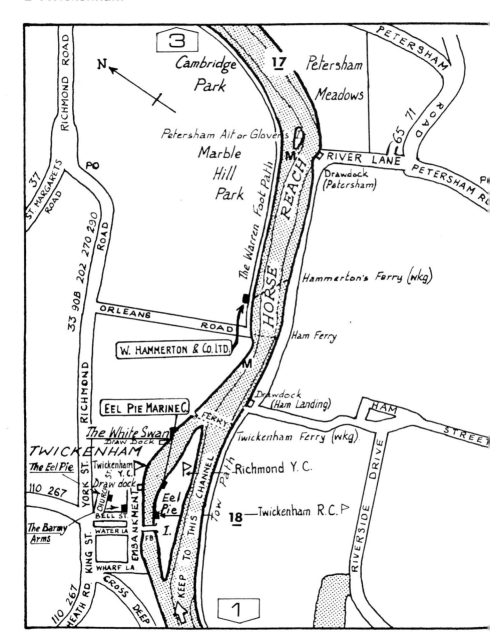

British Motor Yacht Club
Ferry Road, Teddington, Middx (01-977 5710)

Cruising Club (ATYC)

Draw Docks
Ferry Road, Teddington
Ham Dock, Ham Fields Towpath

Towing Path
Surrey Bank, continuous from Teddington Locks and above

Tide End Cottage *(Inn)* 8, Ferry Road, Teddington, Middx (01-977 3634)
The Anglers *(Hotel)* 3, Broom Road, Teddington, Middx (01-977 1517)

Tidal Constants on London Bridge		Mean Tidal Ranges	
HWS + 1 hr 18m ⎱		Springs	8'6"
LWS * — ⎰	at Teddington Lock		2.56m
HWN + 1 hr 08m ⎱		Neaps	4'6"
LWN * — ⎰			1.37m

Duration of Rise and Fall of Average Spring and Neap Tides			
Flood		Ebb	
Springs	**Neaps**	**Springs**	**Neaps**
*2 hrs 00m	*2 hrs 00m	*2 hrs 00m	*2 hrs 00m

Ebb tide sets toward	
Reach	Bank
Horse Reach to Petersham Ait	Middlesex
Petersham Ait to Richmond Railway Br.	Surrey

*The sluices at Richmond Lock maintain this section above a tidal level of 5'9", termed *half-tide*. The tide therefore only rises and falls when the sluices are open. The tidal level therefore remains static for about 8 hrs 15 m over Low Water Springs and 8 hrs 45 m over Low Water Neaps.

CHART DIRECTORY
For key to letter references see p. 21

Eel Pie Marine Limited
Eel Pie Marine Centre, Eel Pie Island,
Twickenham, Middx (01-892 3626)

Boatyard (DIY)
(C, E, L, M, R, S, U, W)

Eel Pie Island Slipways Ltd
Eel Pie Island, Twickenham, Middx (01-891 4481)

Boatyard
(E, M, R)

Cruisemaster Limited
Eel Pie Island, Twickenham, Middx (01-891 1065)

Boatyard
(M, R)

Shipshape Ltd
49, Church Street, Twickenham, Middx
(01-892 3558)

Chandlery
(C)

Moorings at Teddington

Richmond Footbridge

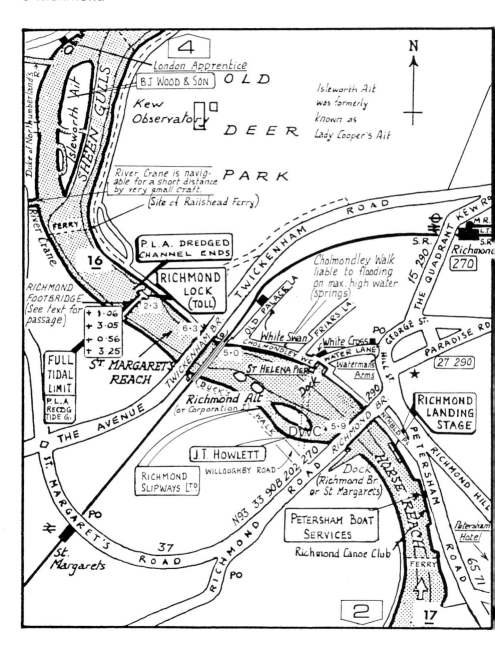

Tidal Constants on London Bridge		Mean Tidal Ranges	
HWS + 1 hr 06m		Springs	16'0''
LWS + 3 hr 05m	at Richmond Lock	*Below lock*	4.88m
HWN + 0 hr 56m		Neaps	12'0''
LWN + 3 hr 25m		*Below lock*	3.66m

Duration of Rise and Fall of Average Spring and Neap Tides

Flood		*Ebb*	
Springs	**Neaps**	**Springs**	**Neaps**
3 hrs 30m	4 hrs 00m	8 hrs 45m	8 hrs 45m

Ebb tide sets toward

Reach	*Bank*
Horse Reach	Surrey
St Margarets Reach	Middlesex
Sheen Gulls	Middlesex

CHART DIRECTORY
For key to letter references see p. 21

Richmond Lock (PLA)
(01-940 0634)

Lock-keeper's Office
(This office also deals with
enquiries for PLA moorings
in the Upper Tideway)

J. T. Howlett
Duck's Walk, Willoughby Road, East Twickenham,
Middx (01-892 3183)

Boatyard
(C, D, G, M, W)

Richmond Slipways Ltd
1, Duck's Walk, East Twickenham, Middx
(01-892 5062)

Boatyard
(B, G, R, M, W)

Petersham Boat Services
Petersham Road, Richmond, Surrey (01-940 0173)

Self-Drive Hire
(H, M, P, W)

B. J. Wood and Son
Isleworth Ait, Isleworth, Middx (01-560 4848)

Boatyard
(R)

Richmond Canoe Club
Lansdowne Boathouse, Petersham Road,
Richmond, Surrey (01-940 9898)

Canoe club

Richmond Landing Stage (TWA)
Thames Passenger Services (01-940 2244)

*Landing for passenger vessels.
Private craft by arrangement.*

St Helena Pier (Private)
R J Turk & Sons
Thames Side, Kingston-on-Thames,
Surrey (01-546 2434/5775)

*Landing for charter craft
operated by lessee.*

Draw Docks
Richmond Bridge Draw Dock, Twickenham side
Water Lane Draw Dock, Water Lane, Richmond
Isleworth Draw Dock, Isleworth Parish Church (by *London Apprentice*)

Towing Path
From Orleans Road (Chart 2) on the Middlesex Bank downstream to Petersham Ferry.
From Richmond Road Bridge downstream on the Surrey Bank.
Petersham Ferry to Richmond Road Bridge – *No Towing Path.*

Petersham Hotel *(Hotel & Restaurant),* Richmond Hill, Richmond (01-940 7471)
The Britannia *(Inn),* 5, Brewers Lane, Richmond (01-940 1071)
The Waterman's Arms, 12, Water Lane, Richmond (01-940 2893)
White Cross Hotel *(Inn),* Water Lane, Richmond (01-940 0909)
White Swan *(Inn),* Old Palace Lane, Richmond (01-940 0959)
The London Apprentice *(Inn),* 62, Church Street, Isleworth, Middx (01-560 3538)

Notes
For tidal information above Richmond Lock, see previous chart.
For passage of Richmond Sluices or Lock, see page 25.
For details of angling between Teddington and Yantlet Creek apply to:
Senior Fishery Officer, Thames Water Authority, Rivers House, Crossness Sewage Treatment
Works, Abbey Wood, London, SE2 9AQ (01-310 5500), (also covers Rivers Darent and Cray).

Tidal Constants on London Bridge		Mean Tidal Ranges	
HWS + 1 hr 00m		Springs	17'0"
LWS + 2 hr 59m	at Brentford Creek		5.18m
HWN + 0 hr 50m		Neaps	13'0"
LWN + 3 hr 19m			3.96m

Duration of Rise and Fall of Average Spring and Neap Tides			
Flood		*Ebb*	
Springs	**Neaps**	**Springs**	**Neaps**
3 hr 45m	4 hr 00m	8 hr 45m	8 hr 45m

Ebb tide sets toward	
Reach	*Bank*
Syon Reach downstream to 15 mile mark, opposite Syon House	Middlesex
Syon House to Brentford Dock	Surrey
Brentford Creek downstream	Middlesex

CHART DIRECTORY
For key to letter references see p. 21

T. Norris (Industries) Ltd
6 Wood Lane, Isleworth, TW7 5EA
(01-560 3453 & 01-568 4888)

Chandlers and Marine Engineers.

Brentford Dock Marina
Brentford Marine Sales Ltd, The Boathouse,
Justin Close, Brentford Dock Marina, Brentford,
Middx TW8 8QQ (01-568 0287)
(VHF Ch 14, 16 manned 1000 to 1800)

Boatyard & Sales
(C, E, I, M, R, S, T, U, W)
Entry obtainable 2½ hrs
either side HW. Beam max
16'0" (4.88m)

E. C. Jones & Son (Brentford) Ltd
Brentside Wharf, Dock Road, Brentford, Middx
TW8 8AQ (01-560 7494)

*Boatbuilders & Marine
Engineers*
(B, E, R)

For other services in this area see the Directory Section to Chart 21.

4 Brentford

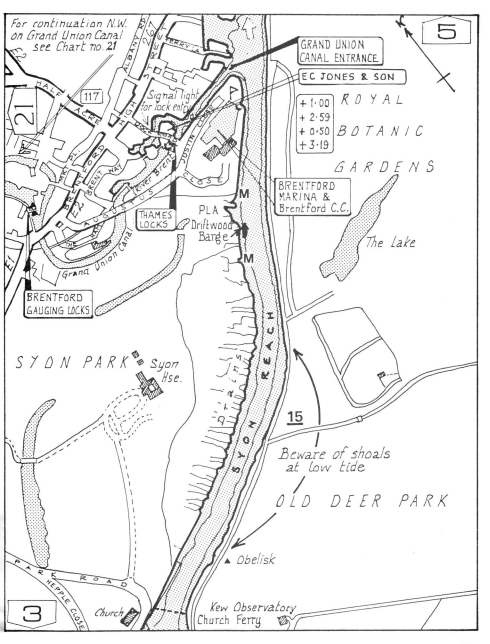

For continuation N.W.
on Grand Union Canal
see Chart no. 21

21

117

HALF ACRE

HIGH STREET

ALBANY RD

BRENTFORD

BRENT WAY

DOCK ROAD

Signal light
for lock entry

AUGUSTUS

River Brent

JUSTIN CLOSE

CLOSE

THAMES
LOCKS

PLA
Driftwood
Barge

Grand Union Canal

BRENTFORD
GAUGING LOCKS

Grand Union

GRAND UNION
CANAL ENTRANCE

EC JONES & SON

+ 1·00
+ 2·59
+ 0·50
+ 3·19

R O Y A L

B O T A N I C

G A R D E N S

BRENTFORD
MARINA &
Brentford C.C.

M

M

The Lake

S Y O N   P A R K   Syon
Hse.

S Y O N   R E A C H

15

Beware of shoals
at low tide

O L D   D E E R   P A R K

PARK ROAD

HEPPLE CLOSE

3

Church

▲ Obelisk

Kew Observatory
Church Ferry

5

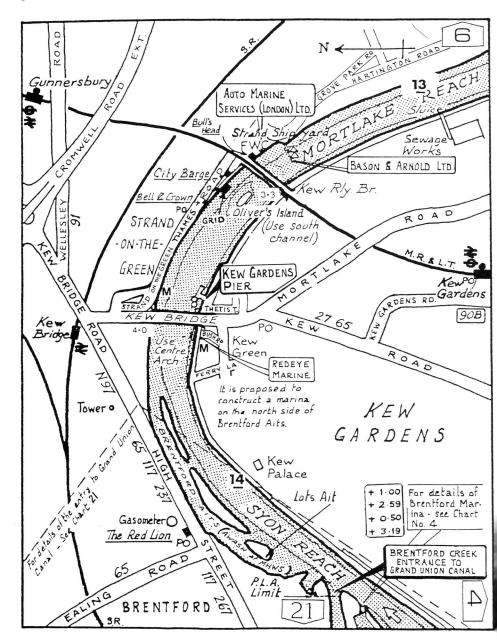

Towing Path
Continuous on the Surrey Bank.

For entry to the Grand Union Canal see text at the commencement of this Section, also preamble to Section 5 on page 92.

Tidal Constants on London Bridge		Mean Tidal Ranges	
HWS + 1 hr 00m ⎫		Springs	17′0″
LWS + 2 hr 59m ⎪ at Brentford Creek			5.18m
HWN + 0 hr 50m ⎬		Neaps	13′0″
LWN + 3 hr 19m ⎭			3.96m

Duration of Rise and Fall of Average Spring and Neap Tides			
Flood		*Ebb*	
Springs	**Neaps**	**Springs**	**Neaps**
3 hr 45m	4 hr 00m	8 hr 45m	8 hr 45m

Ebb tide sets toward	
Reach	*Bank*
Syon Reach (from Brentford Creek) into Mortlake Reach	Middlesex

CHART DIRECTORY

For key to letter references see p. 21

Redeye Marine
Bush Road, Kew Green, Richmond (01-940 8364)

Moorings

Bason and Arnold Limited
Strand Shipyard, 76, Grove Park Road, Chiswick,
London, W4 (01-994 2100/2431/6396)

Boatyard
(B, C, D, E, G, L, M, P, R, T, W)

Auto Marine Services
(see above under Bason & Arnold)

Kew Gardens Pier (TWA)
(01-940 7632)
      Thames Passenger Services:
      (01-940 3891)

Landing for passenger craft.
Private craft only by
arrangement.
(M, W)

Towing Path
Continuous on the Surrey Bank.

City Barge *(Inn)* 27, Strand-on-the-Green, W4 (01-994 2148)
Bull's Head *(Inn)* Strand-on-the-Green, W4 (01-994 0647/1204)
Bell and Crown *(Inn)* 72, Strand-on-the-Green, W4 (01-994 4164)

Note Navigate with extreme care in the vicinity of Lots and Brentford Aits. Do not go inside the aits except on a rising tide within two hours of High Water. Use the centre arch of Kew Bridge when proceeding downstream to avoid any vessels arriving at, or leaving Kew Pier.

Do not use the channel on the Middlesex side of Oliver's Island, except at around HW. This passage is not particularly advisable downstream even then in view of the proximity of Bason and Arnold's pier.

For entry to the Grand Union Canal see text at the commencement of this Section, also preamble to Section 5 on page 92.

PUBLIC TRANSPORT SERVICES

Railway Services

Station	Region or line	Route	*Normal Frequency
Teddington	SR	Waterloo — Kingston	20 mins
Twickenham	SR	Waterloo — Staines	20 mins
St Margarets†	SR	Waterloo — Staines	20 mins
Richmond	SR	Waterloo — Staines	20 mins
Richmond	MR	N. London Line — Richmond	20 mins
Brentford Central	SR	Waterloo — Hounslow	30 mins
Kew Bridge	SR	Waterloo — Hounslow	30 mins
Gunnersbury	LT	District (Richmond)	15 mins
Gunnersbury	MR	N. London Line — Richmond	20 mins
Kew Gardens	LT	District (Richmond)	20 mins
Kew Gardens	MR	N. London Line — Richmond	20 mins
Richmond	LT	District (Richmond)	15 mins

*Not necessarily on Sundays.
†Station closed on Sundays.

London Bus Services

Bus route numbers are shown along principal main roads shown on the charts. Bus route terminals are shown with the route number boxed.

Route No.	Termini	Route No.	Termini
27	Archway Station and Richmond	117	Brentford and Staines
33	Fulwell and Kensington	202	Heathrow and Richmond
37	Peckham and Hounslow	237	Shepherd's Bush and Sunbury
65	Chessington Zoo and Ealing	267	Hampton Court Station and Hammersmith
71	Chessington Zoo and Richmond	270	Richmond Station and Hampton
90B	Kew Gardens Station and Yeading	281	Hounslow and Tolworth
91	Wandsworth Bridge and Hounslow	285	Heathrow Airport Central and Kingston
110	Twickenham Station and Hounslow	290	Staines and Hammersmith

Flat Fare Routes (Pay as you enter)		All-Night Bus Services	
E1	Greenford and Brentford	N93	Fulwell and Hampstead Heath
E2	Greenford and Brentford	N97	Liverpool Street Station and Heathrow

Section 2 **Kew to Wandsworth**

THERE IS A SPEED LIMIT ABOVE WANDSWORTH BRIDGE OF 8 KNOTS (9mph) THROUGH THE WATER

As we approach London, the river is becoming busier with perhaps a small amount of commercial traffic making for Brentford.

Opposite Duke's Meadows on the Middlesex bank is the Mortlake brewery standing on the Surrey shore. From here on craft may encounter rowing eights and fours, practising from the clubs at Hammersmith and Putney. Care should therefore be exercised when negotiating Chiswick and Hammersmith Bridges.

Shoals off Small Profits Draw Dock on the Surrey bank, just below Barnes Railway Bridge should be avoided at low water.

A landing at Hammersmith Pier may be made by arrangement with the lessee. More permanent moorings may also be arranged on application.

There are numerous rowing and sailing clubs stationed along Putney Embankment. Moorings may be available by arrangement with the pier-master or the yard shown in the directory, as well as at the Hurlingham Yacht Club, which is located below Fulham Rail Bridge, on the Surrey Bank.

The mandatory speed limit of 8 knots finishes at Wandsworth Bridge. However, masters of craft should note that excessive speeding below this point, which creates undue wash, or causes damage or annoyance to other river users or the owners of shore property or moored craft is actionable. The Port of London Authority advise that damage may be caused by any craft exceeding 10 knots and that fines for causing damage by speeding can be exacted up to £1,000.

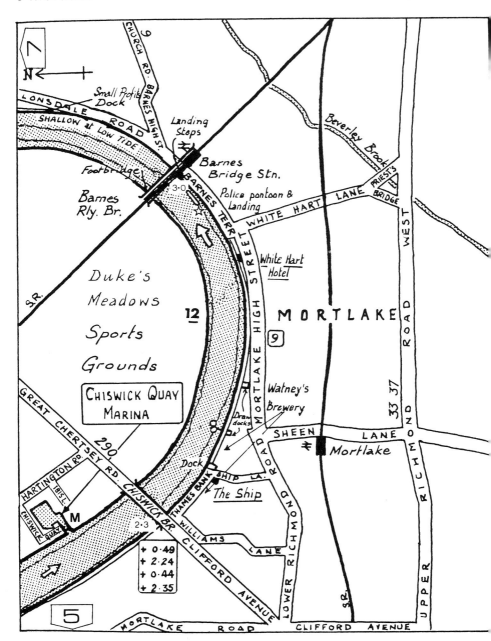

Tidal Constants on London Bridge		Mean Tidal Ranges	
HWS + 0 hr 49m		Springs	17'6"
LWS + 2 hr 24m			5.33m
HWN + 0 hr 44m	at Chiswick Br.	Neaps	13'6"
LWN + 2 hr 35m			4.11m

Duration of Rise and Fall of Average Spring and Neap Tides

Flood		Ebb	
Springs	**Neaps**	**Springs**	**Neaps**
4 hrs 00m	4 hrs 30m	8 hrs 30m	8 hrs 00m

Ebb tide sets toward

Reach	Bank
Mortlake Reach to Chiswick Bridge	Middlesex
Chiswick Bridge to Barnes Bridge	Surrey

CHART DIRECTORY
For key to letter references see p. 21

Metropolitan Police
Thames Division, Barnes
Refer calls to Waterloo Pier (01-434 5411/2)

Police Patrols

Chiswick Quay Marina
Lock Gates, 24 Chiswick Quay, London, W4
(01-994 8743)

Moorings, Marina, Boatyard
(C, D, G, M, R, W)
Entry and departure approx 2
hours either side of HW at Chiswick
Bridge. Max. draught: 4'6" Max.
beam: 15'0".

Barnes Terrace

Landing Steps

Drawdocks
Ship Draw Dock, Ship Lane
Small Profits Draw Dock, Lonsdale Road

Surrey Bank
Surrey Bank

Towing Path
Continuous on the Surrey Bank.

White Hart Hotel, The Terrace, London, SW13 (01-876 5177)
The Ship (*Inn*), Mortlake Riverside, London, SW14 (01-876 1439)

7 Chiswick

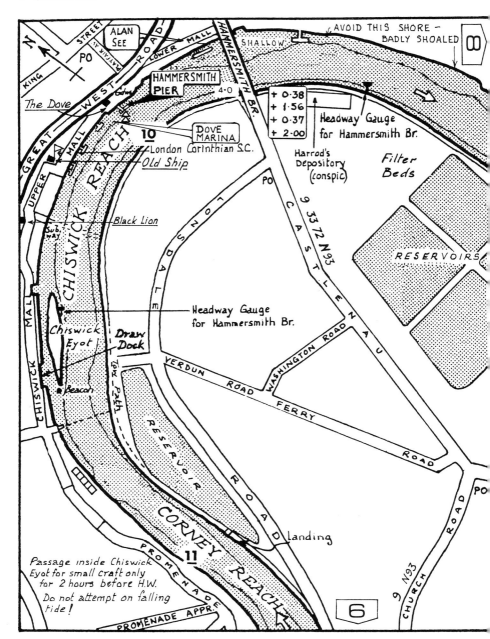

AVOID THIS SHORE —
BADLY SHOALED

SHALLOW

ALAN
SEE

PO

STREET

LOWER MALL

HAMMERSMITH BR.

HAMMERSMITH
PIER

4·0

+ 0·38
+ 1·56
+ 0·37
+ 2·00

Headway Gauge
for Hammersmith Br.

The Dove

WEST MALL

GREAT MALL

UPPER MALL

DOVE
MARINA

London Corinthian S.C.

Old Ship

10

Harrod's
Depository
(conspic)

*Filter
Beds*

PO

9 33 72 N93

CHISWICK REACH

Black Lion

Sub.
way

LONSDALE

CASTELNAU

RESERVOIRS

Headway Gauge
for Hammersmith Br.

Chiswick
Eyot

Draw
Dock

Tow Path

Beacon

WASHINGTON ROAD

CHISWICK MALL

VERDUN ROAD

FERRY

ROAD

Reservoir

landing

ROAD

CORNEY REACH

PROMENADE

11

Passage inside Chiswick
Eyot for small craft only
for 2 hours before H.W.
Do not attempt on falling
tide!

PROMENADE APPR.

6

CHURCH ROAD

9 N93

PO

Tidal Constants on London Bridge — Mean Tidal Ranges

Tidal Constants on London Bridge		Mean Tidal Ranges	
HWS + 0 hr 38m LWS + 1 hr 56m HWN + 0 hr 37m LWN + 2 hr 00m	} at Hammersmith Bridge	Springs Neaps	18'6" 5.63m 14'0" 4.27m

Duration of Rise and Fall of Average Spring and Neap Tides

Flood		Ebb	
Springs	**Neaps**	**Springs**	**Neaps**
4 hrs 15m	5 hrs 00m	8 hrs 00m	7 hrs 30m

Ebb tide sets toward

Reach	*Bank*
Corney Reach	Surrey
Chiswick Reach	Middlesex

CHART DIRECTORY

For key to letter references see p. 21

Cooper's Fishing Tackle
204–206 King Street, Hammersmith (01-748 6920)

Shop
(A)

Alan See
Barge 'Elsie', Lower Mall, Hammersmith, W6
(01-748 7738)

Boatyard
(M, R)

Dove Marina
Upper Mall, Hammersmith, W6 (01-748 7454)

Moorings
(M, W)

Hammersmith Pier
(01-748 8607)

Privately Leased. Landing and mooring by prior arrangement only.

London Corinthian S.C.
Linden House, Upper Mall, London, W6
(01-748 3280)

Sailing Club

Draw Docks
Chiswick Draw Dock, Chiswick Mall

Towing Path
Continuous on the Surrey Bank.

The Black Lion, 2, South Black Lion Lane, Hammersmith (01-748 7056)
The Dove, 19, Upper Mall, Hammersmith (01-748 5405)
The Old Ship *(Inn)*, 25, Upper Mall, Hammersmith (01-748 2886/2593)

Note. Restricted headroom and channel width at Hammersmith Bridge. For further details see pages 16, 18 and 19.
Headroom gauges are located at Chiswick Eyot and Harrods Depository.
Keep clear of Middlesex bank, which is shallow.

8 Putney

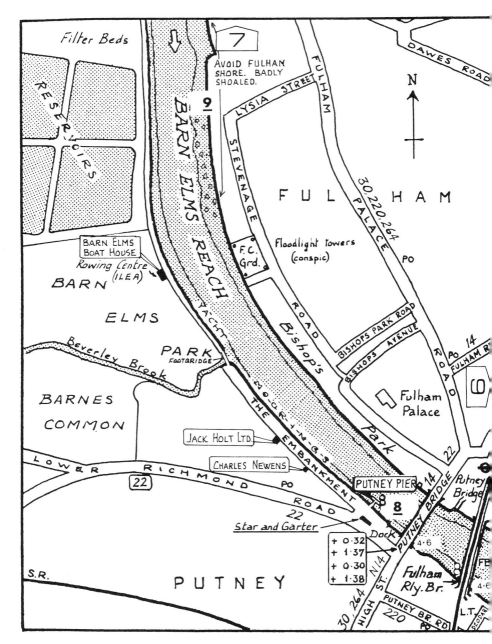

Tidal Constants on London Bridge		Mean Tidal Ranges	
HWS + 0 hr 32m		Springs	19'3"
LWS + 1 hr 37m	at Putney Bridge		5.87m
HWN + 0 hr 30m		Neaps	14'6"
LWN + 1 hr 38m			4.42m

Duration of Rise and Fall of Average Spring and Neap Tides

Flood		Ebb	
Springs	**Neaps**	**Springs**	**Neaps**
4 hrs 30m	5 hrs 15m	8 hrs 00m	7 hrs 15m

Ebb tide sets toward

Reach	Bank
Barn Elms Reach (Hammersmith Bridge to 9 mile mark)	Middlesex
Barn Elms Reach to Fulham Railway Bridge	Surrey

CHART DIRECTORY
For key to letter references see p. 21

Putney Pier (TWA)
(01-788 5104)

Landing.
(L)

    Thames Passenger Services
    (01-788 6822)

Barn Elms Boat House
Putney Towpath, London, SW15 (01-788 9472)

Moorings
(M, W)

Charles Newens Marine Co.
Putney Embankment, London, SW15 (01-788 4587)

Boatyard
(C, E, R, F, M, W)

Jack Holt Limited
Putney Embankment, London, SW15 (01-788 9255)

Chandlery

Drawdocks
Putney Draw Dock, Putney Bridge

Upstream side, Surrey Bank.

Towing Path
There is a towing path on the Surrey Bank from Hammersmith Bridge to the upstream side of Beverley Brook.

Star and Garter Hotel, The Embankment, Putney (01-788 0345).
(A) **Tooke's Tackle,** 614 Fulham Road, SW6 (01-736 1484) (Fishing tackle).

Warning
A large number of sailing (dinghy racing) and rowing clubs are located in this area. Remember that powered craft must give way to sailing and rowing craft.

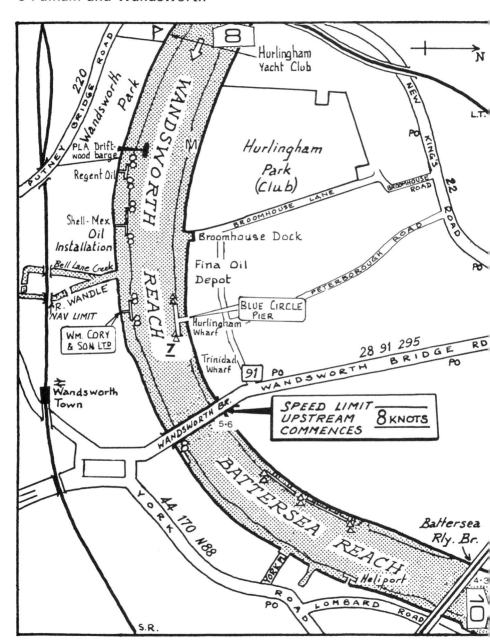

Tidal Constants on London Bridge		Mean Tidal Ranges	
HWS + 0 hr 32m ⎫		Springs	19'3"
LWS + 1 hr 37m ⎪ at Putney Bridge			5.87m
HWN + 0 hr 30m ⎬		Neaps	14'6"
LWN + 1 hr 38m ⎭			4.42m

Duration of Rise and Fall of Average Spring and Neap Tides

Flood		Ebb	
Springs	**Neaps**	**Springs**	**Neaps**
4 hrs 30m	5 hrs 15m	8 hrs 00m	7 hrs 15m

Ebb tide sets toward

Reach	Bank
Wandsworth Reach	Surrey
Battersea Reach as far as Battersea Bridge	Surrey

CHART DIRECTORY

For key to letter references see p. 21

Hurlingham Yacht Club
Deodar Road, Putney (01-788 5547)

Yacht Club.
(M)

Towing Path
There is no towing path below Putney.

Note: The mandatory speed limit of 8 knots ends at Wandsworth Bridge. However all craft must operate at a speed which does not cause excessive wash to the hindrance of other river users, or riparian owners. Navigation of the River Wandle is possible at certain states of the tide by small craft as far as the railway bridge.

Caution: The MV *Blue Circle Enterprise* makes regular deliveries of cement to the Blue Circle Pier off Hurlingham Wharf. Keep well clear if the pier is in use.

PUBLIC TRANSPORT SERVICES

Railway Services

Station	Region or line	Route	*Normal Frequency
Mortlake	SR	Waterloo — Staines	20 mins
Barnes Bridge	SR	Waterloo — Hounslow	30 mins
Hammersmith	LT (Met)	Hammersmith & City	8 mins
Hammersmith	LT (Dist)	Ealing Bdwy or Richmond	8 mins
Hammersmith	LT (Picc)	Heathrow or Rayners Lane	5 mins
Putney	SR	Waterloo — Staines	20 mins
Putney Bridge	LT (Dist)	Wimbledon Branch	15 mins
Wandsworth Town	SR	Waterloo — Richmond	20 mins

*Not necessarily on Sundays. On Underground lines the frequency may increase during rush hours on weekdays.

London Bus Services

Bus route numbers are shown along principal main roads shown on the charts. Bus route terminals are shown with the route number boxed.

Route No.	Termini	Route No.	Termini
9	Mortlake and Liverpool Street Station	91	Wandsworth and Hounslow West
14	Hornsey Rise and Putney	170	Wandsworth and Aldwych
22	Putney Common and Homerton	220	Tooting Station and Harlesden
28	Golders Green Station and Wandsworth	264	South Kensington Station and Roehampton
30	Putney Heath and Hackney Wick	290	Hammersmith and Staines
33	Fulwell and Kensington	295	Ladbroke Grove and Clapham Junction
37	Peckham and Hounslow		
44	Mitcham and London Bridge Station	**All-Night Bus Services**	
72	East Acton and Tolworth	N14	Liverpool Street and Kingston
73	Stoke Newington and Hammersmith	N88	Liverpool Street and Wandsworth
74	Camden Town and Putney Heath	N93	Fulwell and Hampstead Heath

Maps and Publications. Free pocket maps of all London Transport's services as well as a special tourist information map are available. Free maps, leaflets and London Transport books can be obtained from any London Transport Enquiry Office. These are at Piccadilly Circus, Oxford Circus, King's Cross, Euston, Victoria and St. James's Park Underground stations. Maps and free leaflets are also available by post from the Public Relations Officer, London Transport, 55 Broadway, SW1H 0BD.

Section 3 **Wandsworth to London Bridge**

A busier stretch of the river compared with the previous sections, where a good deal of commercial traffic may be encountered.

It is also advisable, as anywhere on the Tideway, to keep a sharp lookout for driftwood and rubbish which can wreak havoc on one's propeller or steering gear, if it becomes trapped there.

The PLA provide lighters moored at strategic places with signs displayed for the deposit of driftwood. These lighters may also be used for dry refuse disposal, but not of course, for sewage. Sewage disposal points are few and far between on the Tideway. Those that are available are shown in the Chart Directories, under *Boatyards*.

Oil tankers may be encountered in addition to the trains of lighters being towed behind the fussy little tugs. Give all this traffic a wide berth and always listen out for sound signals from any likely looking moored vessel which is about to leave her berth.

From Westminster Bridge downwards, you are also likely to meet a considerable number of passenger launches.

Lighters on Kings Reach

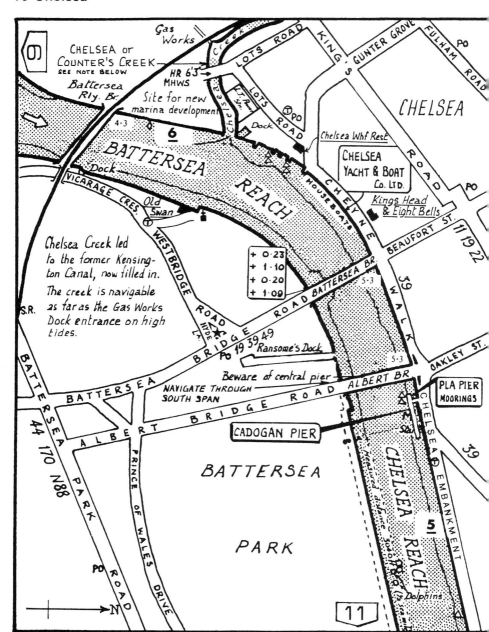

Tidal Constants on London Bridge		Mean Tidal Ranges	
HWS + 0 hr 23m		Springs	20'0"
LWS + 1 hr 10m	at Battersea Bridge		6.10m
HWN + 0 hr 20m		Neaps	14'6"
LWN + 1 hr 09m			4.42m

Duration of Rise and Fall of Average Spring and Neap Tides

Flood		Ebb	
Springs	**Neaps**	**Springs**	**Neaps**
4 hrs 45m	5 hrs 30m	7 hrs 30m	7 hrs 00m

Ebb tide sets toward

Reach	Bank
Battersea Reach (down to Battersea Bridge)	Surrey
Battersea Bridge to Albert Bridge	Middlesex
Chelsea Reach (Upstream end)	Middlesex (slight)
Remainder of reach shown on chart	None

CHART DIRECTORY
For key to letter references see p. 21

Chelsea Yacht and Boat Co. Ltd
Old Ferry Wharf, Cheyne Walk, London, SW10
(01-352 1427)

Boatyard and dry dock
(B, E, G, M)

Cadogan Pier (PLA)
Chelsea Embankment, London, SW10
(01-352 4604)

Landing
(L, M)

Drawdocks
Battersea Church Draw Dock,
Vicarage Crescent, Battersea

South (Surrey) Bank below
Battersea Railway Bridge

Chelsea Wharf Restaurant Unit 4, Lots Road, SW10 (01-351 6205/4363/0861)
Old Swan *(Inn)* 116, Battersea Church Road, SW11 (01-228 7152)
King's Head & Eight Bells *(Rest)* 50, Cheyne Walk, SW3 (01-352 1820)

Notes The beacons on the South (Surrey) Bank, upstream opposite Cadogan Pier Stairs and downstream against Chelsea Bridge are one half of a nautical mile (3,040 feet) apart. A useful check on progress can therefore be made here by timing one's passage between them, and calculating one's speed over the ground in knots.

   Ransome's Dock is no longer used, having been incorporated into a new housing development.

11 Nine Elms

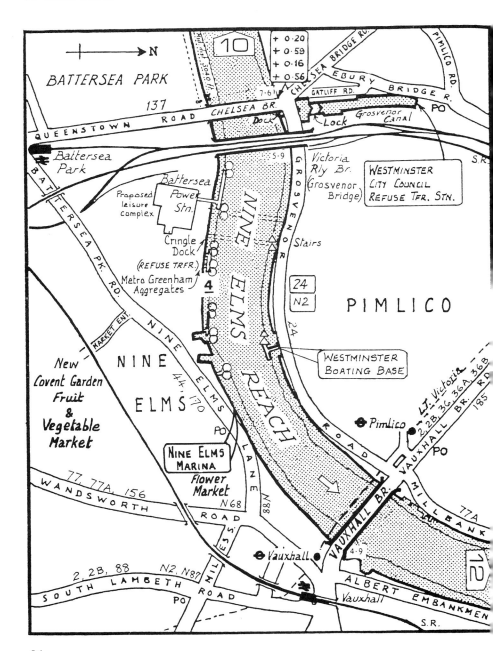

Tidal Constants on London Bridge		Mean Tidal Ranges	
HWS + 0 hr 20m		Springs	19'9"
LWS + 0 hr 59m	at Chelsea Bridge		6.02m
HWN + 0 hr 16m		Neaps	15'0"
LWN + 0 hr 56m			4.57m

Duration of Rise and Fall of Average Spring and Neap Tides			
Flood		*Ebb*	
Springs	**Neaps**	**Springs**	**Neaps**
4 hrs 45m	5 hrs 45m	7 hrs 30m	6 hrs 45m

Ebb tide sets toward	
Reach	*Bank*
Chelsea Bridge to Victoria Railway Bridge	North (Middlesex)
Nine Elms Reach	South (Surrey)

CHART DIRECTORY

For key to letter references see p. 21

Boat Showrooms of London Ltd
286 Kensington High Street, London, W14 (Head
Office) (01-602 0123)

Chandlers and Boat Sales
(C)
Admiralty Chart Agents

Nine Elms Marina
Nine Elms Lane, London, SW8 (01-720 7700)

Moorings
(M, R)

Westminster Boating Base (Pier)
Dinorvic Wharf, 136, Grosvenor Road, SW1
(01-821 7389)

Youth Sailing Club

Grosvenor Canal
Westminster City Council
City Engineer's Department, Grosvenor Canal Depot,
Gatliff Road, SW1 (01-730 1540)

Navigation Authority for canal.
Lock dimensions:
90'0" long × 18'6" beam × 7'0"
draught. Headroom 8'6".
For commercial use by council
only.

Notes: Between Chelsea and Victoria Railway Bridges on the North (Middlesex) Bank is
the entrance to the Grosvenor Canal. A short length of this canal is still in existence and
is used by the WCC as a refuse transfer station. *See note above under 'Grosvenor Canal'.*
Watch out for refuse lighters which may be entering or leaving around High Water.
　　Take care when navigating in the areas of Cringle Dock and Metro Greenham's jetty
as large vessels often manoeuvre in the river when calling or leaving these installations.
　　Be prepared to meet small sailing craft off the Westminster Boating Base pier.

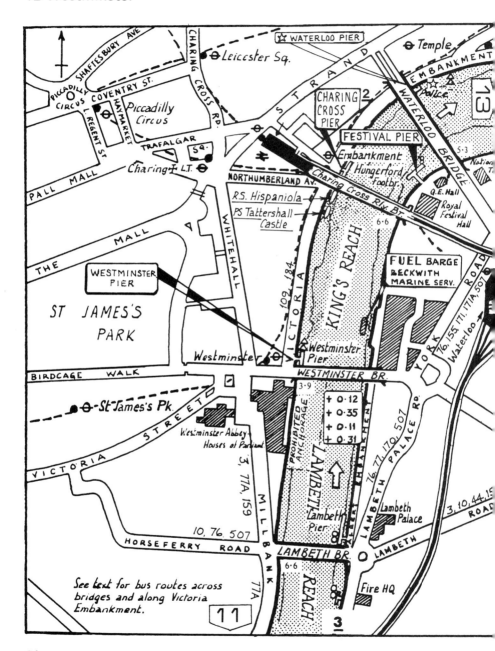

Tidal Constants on London Bridge			Mean Tidal Ranges	
HWS	+ 0 hr 12m		Springs	21'0"
LWS	+ 0 hr 35m			6.41m
HWN	+ 0 hr 11m	at Westminster Bridge	Neaps	15'0"
LWN	+ 0 hr 31m			4.57m

Duration of Rise and Fall of Average Spring and Neap Tides			
Flood		**Ebb**	
Springs	**Neaps**	**Springs**	**Neaps**
5 hrs 15m	6 hrs 00m	7 hrs 15m	6 hrs 30m

Ebb tide sets toward	
Reach	*Bank*
Lambeth Reach	South (Surrey)
King's Reach	North (Middlesex)

CHART DIRECTORY

For key to letter references see p. 21

Metropolitan Police
Thames (River) Division, Waterloo Pier
(01-434 5411/2)
(VHF Ch 14, 16: Call sign *THAMES POLICE*)

Police Patrols

Lambeth Pier
Albert Embankment

Private

Beckwith Marine Services (Fuel) Ltd
Barge *Freddy,* c/o Westminster Pier, SW1
(01-930 0068)

Refueller barge
(C, D, G, L, P, U, W)

Westminster Pier (TWA)
Victoria Embankment, SW1 (01-930 8294)

Passenger Vessels have
priority

    Passenger Vessel details:

    Downstream services (01-930 4097)
    Upstream services (01-930 2062)
    Thames Barrier cruise (01-930 3373)
                  (01-740 8263)
    Lunch cruises, discos (01-839 2349)
                (01-839 2164/01-722 9132)
    Evening cruises (01-839 2349)
                (01-839 2164/01-722 9132)

Charing Cross Pier (TWA)
Victoria Embankment WC2 (01-839 5393)
    Passenger Vessel details:

Passenger Vessels have
priority

    Tower and Greenwich (01-930 0970)

Captain O. M. Watts Ltd
45 Albemarle Street, London, W1 (01-493 4633)

Chandlers and Chart Agents
Admiralty Chart Agents

Arthur Beale Ltd
194, Shaftesbury Avenue, London WC2
(01-836 9034)

Chandlers

Force 4 Chandlery
30, Bressenden Place, Buckingham Palace Rd.
London SW1E 5DB (01-828 3900/3382)

Clothing and Chandlery

PS 'Tattershall Castle'
Victoria Embankment, SW1 (01-839 6548)

Restaurant Ship, moored upstream of
Charing Cross Railway Bridge on
North Bank.

RS 'Hispaniola'
Victoria Embankment, WC2
(01-839 3011/5769)

Restaurant Ship, moored upstream of
Charing Cross Railway Bridge on
North Bank.

Festival Pier (TWA)
South Bank, SE1 (01-261 0455)
    Passenger Vessel details:
    Luncheon cruises (summer only)
    (01-839 2349)

Moorings
(L, M, S, U, W)

London Tourist Board
River Trip Passenger Enquiries, 4 Grosvenor
Gardens, London, SW1 (01-730 4812)

*General enquiry service for passenger trips
from all piers.*

Warning: *There is a prohibition on mooring or anchoring in the fairway adjacent to the
Houses of Parliament.*

Westminster Bridge from Victoria Embankment

Kensington Canal 1977   *Photo: Derek Pratt*

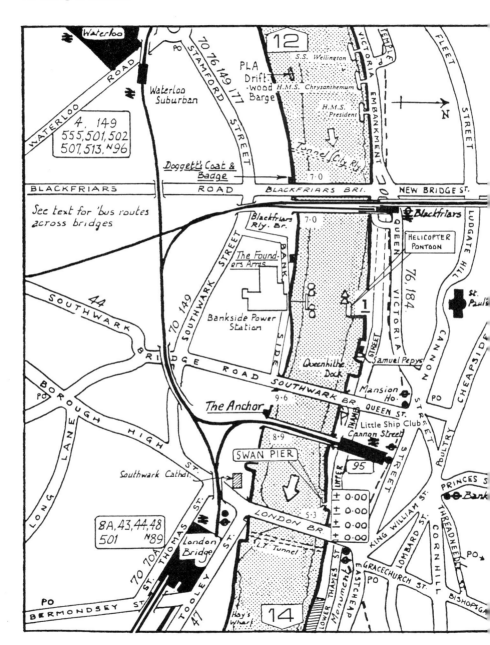

Tidal Constants on London Bridge		Mean Tidal Ranges	
HWS ± 0 hr 00m		Springs	21'6''
LWS ± 0 hr 00m	at London Bridge		6.56m
HWN ± 0 hr 00m		Neaps	15'3''
LWN ± 0 hr 00m			4.65m

Duration of Rise and Fall of Average Spring and Neap Tides			
Flood		*Ebb*	
Springs	**Neaps**	**Springs**	**Neaps**
5 hrs 30m	6 hrs 15m	6 hrs 45m	6 hrs 15m

Ebb tide sets toward	
Reach	*Bank*
King's Reach and Upper Pool (at Tower Bridge)	North (Middlesex)

CHART DIRECTORY
For key to letter references see p. 21

H.M. Customs and Excise (See page 204)
Lower Thames Street, Custom House,
London, EC3R 6EE (01-626 1515)

Collector of Customs, Shipping Registrar, Receiver of Wrecks, Notices to Mariners, etc.
For Customs clearance on arrival or departure.

Little Ship Club
Bell Wharf Lane, EC4 (01-236 7729)
Members (01-248 8318)

Sailing/Cruising Club (ATYC)

London Yacht Centre Ltd
13 Artillery Lane, Bishopsgate, E1
(01-247 0521/9924)

Chandlers, etc.
(C, G, also charts and books)
Admiralty Chart Agents

Edward Stanford Ltd (George Philip Group)
12 Long Acre, WC2 (01-836 1321)

Chart Publishers and Ordnance Survey Agents

J. D. Potter Ltd
145 Minories, EC3N 1NH
(01-709 9076/01-488 0351)

Admiralty Chart Agents and nautical booksellers

The Doggett's Coat and Badge *(Inn)*, Blackfriars Bridge, London, SE1 (01-633 9056)
Restaurant (01-633 9081)
The Tiger Tavern *(Inn)*, 1 Tower Hill, London, EC3 (01-626 5097/5143/5026)
The Anchor *(Inn)*, 1 Bankside, London, SE1 (01-407 1577 – Rest. 01-407 3003)
The Founders Arms, Bankside, SE1 (01-633 9748)
The Samuel Pepys, Brooks Wharf, Upper Thames Street, EC4 (01-248 3048)

PUBLIC TRANSPORT SERVICES
Railway Services

Station	Region or line	Route	*Normal Frequency
Battersea Park	SR	Victoria – Clapham Junction	20 mins
Vauxhall	SR	Waterloo	20 mins
Vauxhall	LT	Victoria Line	5–7 mins
Pimlico	LT	Victoria Line	5–7 mins
Waterloo†	SR	Terminus for Surrey, South & West of England	–
Waterloo	LT	Northern (West End Branch)	6 mins
		Bakerloo	3 mins
Waterloo	SR	City Branch to Bank (Closed Sat noon to **Monday am**)	20 mins
Westminster	LT	Circle/District	6/8 mins
Charing Cross	SR	Terminus for SE London & Kent	–
Embankment	LT	Northern (West End Branch)	
		Bakerloo	6/8 mins
		Circle/District	each
Charing Cross		Northern (West End)	
	LT	Bakerloo	**6/8 mins**
		Jubilee	each
Temple	LT	Circle/District	6/8 mins
Blackfriars††	SR	Terminus for Kent & Mid-Surrey	–
Blackfriars	LT	Circle/District	6/8 mins
Mansion House	LT	Circle/District	6/8 mins
Cannon Street	SR	See Charing Cross (SR) (Closed on Sats and Suns)	–
Cannon Street**	LT	Circle/District	6/8 mins
London Bridge†	SR	Terminus for Mid-Surrey and West Sussex	–
London Bridge	LT	Northern (City Branch)	5–6 mins
Monument	LT	Circle/District	6/8 mins
Bank	LT	Northern (City Branch)	5–6 mins
		Central Line	3/4 mins

*Not necessarily on Sundays or at 'off-peak' times.

†The suburban stations are served from Charing Cross (SR) q.v.

**Restricted opening hours.

††Station closed on Saturdays and Sundays.

London Bus Services

As far as has been practicable bus route numbers have been shown along principal main roads on the charts. Bus route terminals are shown with the route number boxed. Due to the concentration of routes in the Central London area, however, the route numbers omitted from the charts are shown below in relation to the Victoria Embankment and the bridges downstream from Vauxhall Bridge in this Section.

Victoria Embankment
109, 184.

Vauxhall Bridge
2, 2B, 36, 36A, 36B, 77, 77A, 185, N2, N79, N87.
Lambeth Bridge
3, 10, 149, 159, 507, N50, N51, N56, N68.
Westminster Bridge
12, 53, 76, 109, 170, 172, 184, N51, N87, N88, N96.
Waterloo Bridge
1, 4, 68, 155, 171, 176, 188, 199, 501, 502, 513, 555, N14, N18, N50, N78, N89, N94.
Blackfriars Bridge
45, 63, 76, 109, 141, N72, N77, N82, N85, N86.
Southwark Bridge
18, 95, 149, 184.
London Bridge
8A, 10, 21, 35, 40, 43, 47, 48, 133, 501, 513, N47, N89.

Route No.	Termini	Route No.	Termini
1	Marylebone and Greenwich	170	Roehampton and Aldwych
2	West Norwood and Baker Street	171	Forest Hill and Tottenham Garage
2B	Crystal Palace and Golders Green	176	Willesden and Forest Hill
3	Crystal Palace and Camden Town	184	New Cross Gate and Trafalgar Square OR
4	Archway and Farringdon Street		Mansion House Station
8A	London Bridge and Old Ford	185	Victoria and Greenwich
10	Victoria and Wanstead	188	Greenwich and Euston
11	Hammersmith and Liverpool Street Station	199	Bromley Common and Trafalgar Square
12	Norwood Junction and Harlesden		
18	Sudbury and Kings Cross	**Red Arrow Limited Stop Services**	
19	Tooting Bec Station and Archway	501	Waterloo Station and London Bridge Station
21	Sidcup Garage and Moorgate	502	Waterloo Station and Liverpool Street Station
22	Putney Common and Homerton	507	Waterloo Station and Victoria Station
24	Hampstead Heath and Pimlico	513	Waterloo Station and London Bridge Station
35	Clapham Common and Hackney	555	Waterloo Station and King's Cross Station
36	Hither Green Station and Victoria		(Circular)
36A	Brockley Rise and Victoria		
36B	Grove Park and Queen's Park Station	**All Night Bus Services**	
39	Putney Bridge Station and Victoria	N2	Friern Barnet and Crystal Palace
40	Herne Hill and Poplar	N14	Kingston and Waterloo Station
43	London Bridge Station and Friern Barnet	N18	Edgware and Waterloo Station
44	Mitcham and London Bridge Station	N47	Victoria and Bromley South
45	South Kensington and Archway	N50	King's Cross and Greenford (Westbound)
47	Shoreditch and Downham	N51	Greenford and King's Cross (Eastbound)
48	London Bridge and Walthamstow Central	N56	King's Cross and Heathrow
49	Streatham Garage and Shepherd's Bush	N68	Ludgate Circus and Sutton Station
53	Camden Town and Plumstead Common	N72	Victoria Station and Dartford
63	Crystal Palace and King's Cross	N74	Bromley North and Victoria
68	Chalk Farm and South Croydon	N77	Victoria and Thamesmead
70	Peckham and Victoria	N78	Victoria and South Croydon
76	Northumberland Park and Victoria	N79	Willesden and Lewisham
77	Aldwych and Streatham	N82	Victoria and Thamesmead
77A	King's Cross and Putney Heath	N84	Becontree Heath and Victoria
95	Streatham Hill and Mansion House Station	N85	Victoria and Grove Park Station
109	Croydon and Victoria Embankment	N86	Victoria and Crystal Palace
133	Liverpool Street Station and Tooting Broadway	N87	Trafalgar Square and Streatham
137	Crystal Palace and Archway Station	N88	Liverpool Street Station and Wandsworth
141	Wood Green and Grove Park	N89	Liverpool Street Station and Uxbridge
149	Ponders End and Waterloo	N90	Victoria and Hammond Street
155	Wimbledon Station, Elephant & Castle and Aldwych	N96	Trafalgar Square and Chingford Station
159	West Hampstead and Thornton Heath		

Tower Bridge open for sailing ship

Section 4 London Bridge to Margaret Ness (Tripcock Point)

The final large-scale Tideway Section of this Guide takes you out of the Upper Pool through Tower Bridge. Deprived of much trade by closure of the up-river docks, such as St Katharine's, London and the Surrey Group; and, since the first edition of this Guide appeared, the Millwall and Royal Groups, there is a certain amount of lighterage traffic, but in recent years there has been an up-surge in the number of passenger craft plying from Westminster, Charing Cross, Tower and Greenwich Piers. The opening of the Thames Barrier has also helped to swell this traffic which relies heavily on the tourist visiting London.

Little traffic is now encountered using the Limehouse Ship Lock to get into the Limehouse Cut and the Lee through the former Regents Canal Dock. The dock, renamed Limehouse Basin, is at present the subject of development plans by the British Waterways Board. Masters of craft wishing to enter the Regents Canal or the Lee Navigation by this route will find the details explained in the relevant Sections dealing with the canal system in that area.

This Section for PLA purposes comes under the control of the Assistant Harbour Master (Upper), whose office is located on Tower Pier (01-481 0720). In his absence, enquiries may be made of the Duty Officer of the Thames Navigation Service at the Thames Barrier (01-855 0315) or by VHF R/T on Channel 14 (Woolwich Radio).

The route finishes in this section at Margaret Ness, a short distance down river from the new Tidal Barrier at Woolwich. Details of transit procedures current at the date of going to press are included on page 82.

If you have used this guide as a means of navigating the Tideway as far as Blackwall with the intention of proceeding to sea, you are bound by Customs and EEC Regulations and should refer to the Appendix at the end of the book for relevant details. It is also advisable for your own safety to make use of the Yacht and Boat Safety Scheme promoted by HM Coastguard with the help of the CG66 Form which they issue. Details of the scheme and the printed cards (CG66) are obtainable from the Coastguard Office: HM Coastguard, MRSC, Hall Lane, Walton on the Naze, Essex (Frinton on Sea (02556) 5518) or from most RYA affiliated yacht clubs. Cards may be available from the sailing and cruising clubs listed in the Directory sections, particularly those from Richmond downwards.

Incoming craft should pay particular attention to the Customs arrangements which for small craft in the Thames have been very much affected by the disappearance of a number of boarding points due to the loss of commercial traffic in the upper river. Clearance procedures, however, have been simplified since the previous edition.

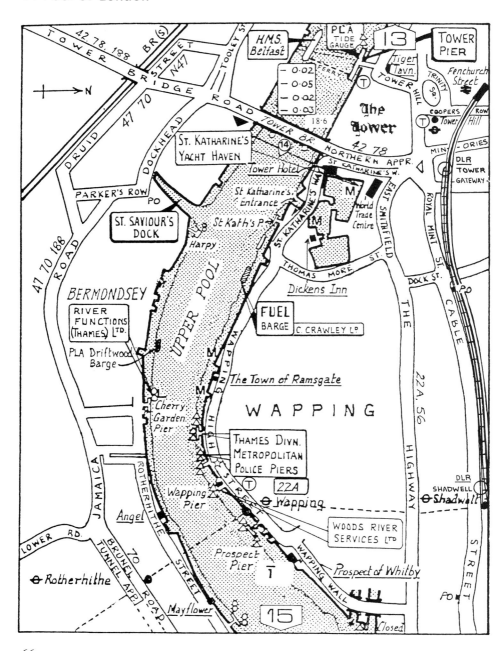

Tidal Constants on London Bridge			Mean Tidal Ranges	
HWS − 0 hr 02m	⎤		Springs	22'0"
LWS − 0 hr 05m	⎬ at Tower Bridge			6.71m
HWN − 0 hr 02m	⎬		Neaps	15'3"
LWN − 0 hr 03m	⎦			4.65m

Duration of Rise and Fall of Average Spring and Neap Tides			
Flood		*Ebb*	
Springs	**Neaps**	**Springs**	**Neaps**
5 hrs 30m	6 hrs 30m	6 hrs 45m	6 hrs 15m

Ebb tide sets toward	
Reach	*Bank*
Upper Pool to Tunnel (Wapping) Pier	South (Surrey)
Below Tunnel (Wapping) Pier	North (Middlesex)

CHART DIRECTORY
For key to letter references see p. 21

*Tower Pier (TWA)
EC3N 4DT (01-481 3800)

Landing by arrangement with Piermaster.

   Passenger Vessel details:
   River Cruises (01-488 0344)
   'Belfast' Ferry (01-858 2752)

   Assistant Harbour Master (Upper), PLA
   Upper Pontoon, Tower Pier, London,
   EC3N 4PL (01-481 0720)

Navigational & Tidal Information
(For details of moorings telephone 01-940 0634)

Tower Bridge
Superintendent Engineer's Office, London, SE1
(01-407 0922/2129)

For enquiries about bridge opening.
(See also details on p. 70)

St Katharine Haven Ltd
52 St Katharine's Way, London, E1 9LB
(01-488 2400) Club (01-481 8286)

Yacht Marina and Club.
(C, D, G, M, P, R, S, T, U, W)
(Details of entry on page 68)

Cruising Association
Ivory House, St Katharine's Dock, London, E1 9AT
(01-481 0881)

General Cruising Organization
Library & Information

Cherry Garden Pier
River Functions (Thames) Ltd, Cherry Garden Street,
SE16 4TU (01-237 5134)

Landing by arrangement.

C. Crawley Ltd
Barge 'Thames Refueller', Hermitage Wharf,
Thomas More Street, London E1 (01-481 1774)

Refuelling Barge moored offshore.
(D, P, W)

Metropolitan Police
Thames Division, 98, Wapping High Street,
London, E1 9NE (01-488 5291)
VHF Channel 14 (Call Sign: *THAMES POLICE*)

Police Patrols.

Wapping (Tunnel) Pier (Private)   *Landing by arrangement.*
Woods River Services Limited, PO Box 177,   (F)
66 Lee Park, London, SE3 9JA (Office)
(01-481 2711/2955)

Pumpkin Marine & Leisure Ltd   *Chandlers*
100, The Highway, London E1 9BX
(01-480 6630)

The Tiger Tavern *(Inn)*, 1 Tower Hill, London, EC3 (01-626 5097)
Tower Hotel, St Katharine's Way, London, E1 9LD (01-481 2575)
The Dickens Inn by the Tower, St Katharine's Way, E1 (01-488 2208)
The Town of Ramsgate, Wapping High Street, E1
The Prospect of Whitby *(Inn)*, Wapping Wall (01-481 1317/1859)
The Angel *(Inn)*, Rotherhithe Street (01-237 3608)
The Mayflower *(Inn)*, Rotherhithe Street (01-237 1898/4088)

*The Upper Pontoon at Tower Pier is occupied by the PLA.

Port of London Authority   *Head Offices*
Europe House, World Trade Centre,
London E1 9AA (01-481 8484)

ENTRY TO ST KATHARINE YACHT HAVEN

Entry is by way of a tidal lock (30'0" × 140'0"). By special arrangement yachts of larger size can be accommodated. The lock is operable two hours either side of High Water (at Tower Bridge), within the hours of 0600 to 2100 in summer and 0800 to 1800 in winter. Lift bridges are sited at the head and tail of the entrance lock. There is a 200'0" long pier in the river by the entrance to the marina for craft arriving outside of these times.

Maximum draught: HWN 11'0"
                 HWS 14'0"

Arrangements must be made in advance by letter or telephone, Harbour Master's telephone number: 01-488 2400.

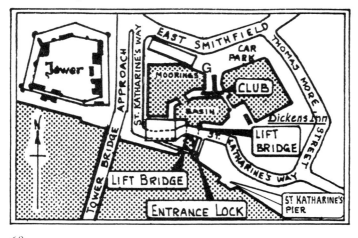

Entering St. Katharine Haven

MOORINGS UNDER THE CONTROL OF THE PLA
Moorings are available in the river off Wapping High Street on the North (Middlesex) Bank.

Details from the Assistant Harbour Master (Upper Section) at the Richmond Lock Office (Tel: 01-940 0634).

TOWER BRIDGE
Passage through Tower Bridge is normally conducted through the central span, which is 200 feet wide. With the bascules closed the headroom varies at the centre of the span between about 28 feet at Mean High Water Springs and 50 feet at Mean Low Water Springs. The draught is never less than $18'6''$, (MLWS).

To gain access to the Upper Pool, masters of yachts and larger craft, requiring to do so, are able to request that the bridge be opened if their vessel is unable to pass the bridge when closed, either due to the air draught being in excess of the above dimensions, or because they are unable to lower or remove funnel, and mast (or masts), or that risk may be occasioned to cargo. (Headroom increased by $111'0''$).

24 hours notice of such passage is required, either in writing or by telephone to:

The Bridge Master, Superintendent Engineer's Office, Tower Bridge, London, SE1 (01-407 0922/2129).

All such passages where required should be arranged during daylight hours, if at all possible. Night operation is costly. Tower Bridge is maintained and operated by the City of London Corporation and not by the Port of London Authority. There is no charge for the service.

Signals by Vessels requiring the bascules to be raised.
Where notice has been given and accepted, on arrival in the proximity of the bridge, the vessel concerned by day should make a sound signal of one prolonged blast followed by two short blasts and one long blast on the horn, siren or whistle. The bridge master should be contacted by VHF R/T in advance of arrival on Channel 14.

Signals displayed to vessels by the bridge master at Tower Bridge.
While the bascules are lowered red light signals on each pier on both sides of the bridge are shown. If the bascules cannot be raised owing to mechanical breakdown or other cause, 4 ft diameter discs bearing black and white diagonal stripes are displayed fourteen feet to landward of the signals. In restricted visibility a high frequency note of 820 cps will be relayed from the north pier of the bridge by loud-hailer. At night the discs will be illuminated.

When the bridge is open (bascules raised), green light signals are displayed from each pier on both sides of the bridge.

At night while the bascules are lowered red lights are displayed from each pier on either side of the bridge. Orange lights at the ends of the bascules are also shown in similar fashion to the other fixed bridges on the tideway. If the bascules are unable to be opened the discs normally shown by day are floodlit.

When the bridge is open (bascules raised), the red lights change to green and the orange lights continue to be shown from the ends of the bascules in their raised positions.

A tide gauge is located at Tower Pier.

The last four bridges down the Thames – Southwark, Cannon Street, London and Tower.

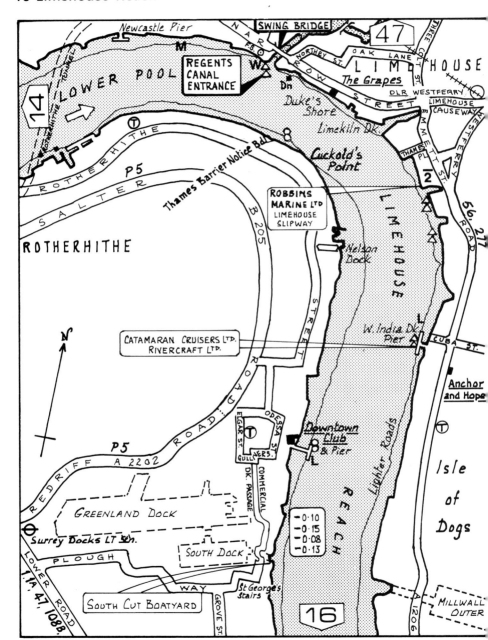

Tidal Constants on London Bridge		Mean Tidal Ranges	
HWS — 0 hr 10m		Springs	22'0"
LWS — 0 hr 15m	at Greenland Entrance		6.71m
HWN — 0 hr 08m		Neaps	15'3"
LWN — 0 hr 13m			4.65m

Duration of Rise and Fall of Average Spring and Neap Tides

Flood		*Ebb*	
Springs	**Neaps**	**Springs**	**Neaps**
5 hrs 30m	6 hrs 30m	6 hrs 45m	6 hrs 00m

Ebb tide sets toward

Reach	*Bank*
Lower Pool of London	North (Middlesex)
Limehouse Reach (Cuckold's Point to West India Dock Pier)	North (Middlesex)
Limehouse Reach (remainder)	South (Surrey)

CHART DIRECTORY

For key to letter references see p. 21

*Limehouse Ship Lock
British Waterways Board, Pierhead Office,
Limehouse Basin, Narrow Street, E14 8DN
(01-790 3444)

Entrance to Limehouse Basin,
Regent's Canal and Limehouse
Cut. See page 143

Limehouse Slipway
Robbins (Marine) Ltd
Bridge Wharf, West Ferry Road, E14
(01-987 5884)

Boatyard
(R)

Rightcraft Marine Services Ltd
3, West Ferry Road, E14 (01-515 2952)

Chandlers

West India Dock Pier (Private)
Catamaran Cruisers Ltd, West India Dock Pier,
Cuba Street, London, E14 8LB (01-987 1185)
(also) Rivercraft Limited (01-515 7345)

Landing by arrangement
(F)

(F)

South Cut Boatyard
Commercial Dock Passage, Gulliver Street, SE16
(01-231 0418)

Boatyard
(M, R)

The Grapes *(Inn)*, 76 Narrow Street, E14 (01-987 4396)
Downtown Club *(Restaurant)*, 4 Odessa Street, SE16 (01-231 8833/0745 or 01-855 1814)
(Mooring at jetty by arrangement)
Anchor and Hope *(Inn)*, 41 Westferry Road, E14 (01-987 3141)

*For tidal constants at tail of the Limehouse Ship Lock consult Chart No. 47 on page 138.

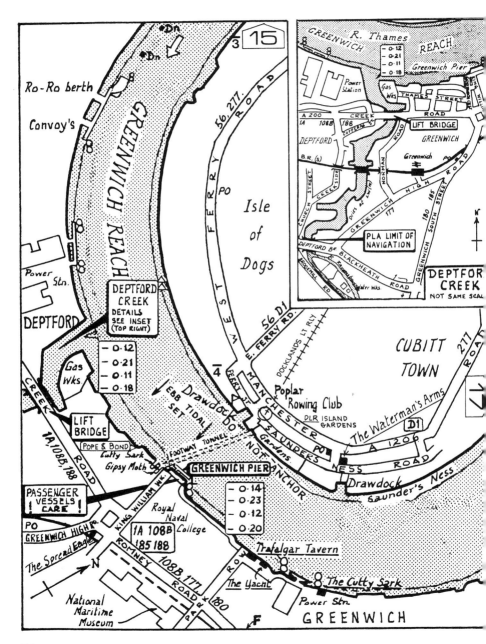

Tidal Constants on London Bridge		Mean Tidal Ranges	
HWS — 0 hr 14m		Springs	21'6"
LWS — 0 hr 23m	at Greenwich Pier		6.56m
HWN — 0 hr 12m		Neaps	15'0"
LWN — 0 hr 20m			4.57m

Duration of Rise and Fall of Average Spring and Neap Tides

Flood		*Ebb*	
Springs	**Neaps**	**Springs**	**Neaps**
5 hrs 45m	6 hrs 30m	6 hrs 45m	6 hrs 00m

Ebb tide sets toward

Reach	*Bank*
Greenwich Reach	South (Surrey)

Warning: The Spring ebb sets hard into Greenwich Pier. Anchoring should be avoided and extreme care taken if mooring at the pier.

CHART DIRECTORY

For key to letter references see p. 21

Greenwich Pier (TWA)
King William Walk, SE10 (01-858 0079)

    Passenger Vessel details:
    Thames Passenger Services (01-858 3996)
    Tower Pier Boat Operators (Greenwich)
    (01-858 6722)

Landing by arrangement

Deptford Creek Lift Bridge
Bridgemaster's Office, Creek Road, SE10
(01-858 5349)

Not permanently manned. Prior notice required for working.

Pope and Bond Limited
32, Wood Wharf, London, SE10 (01-858 0116)

Barge owners & builders
(B, C, E, R)

Greenwich Marine Ltd
22, College Approach, Greenwich, SE10 9HY
(01-858 1446)

Chandlers
(C, G)

East Greenwich Garage Ltd
43, Trafalgar Road, Greenwich, SE10 (01-858 4881)

Auto engineers
Petrol, diesel (DERV)

Poplar, Blackwall & District Rowing Club
Ferry Street, E14 (01-987 3071)

Rowing club

Draw Docks
Johnson's, Poplar (obstructed)
Newcastle (or Christchurch), Poplar

North bank, off Ferry St
North bank, Saunders Ness Rd

The Spread Eagle *(Restaurant)*, 2, Stockwell Street, SE10 (01-853 2333)
Cutty Sark Tavern and Restaurant, Ballast Quay, SE10 9PO (01-858 3146)
Trafalgar Tavern, Park Row, Greenwich, SE10 (01-858 2437)
The Yacht Tavern, 5, Crane Street, Greenwich, SE10 (01-858 0175)
The Waterman's Arms, 1, Glengarnock Avenue, London, E14 (01-538 0712)

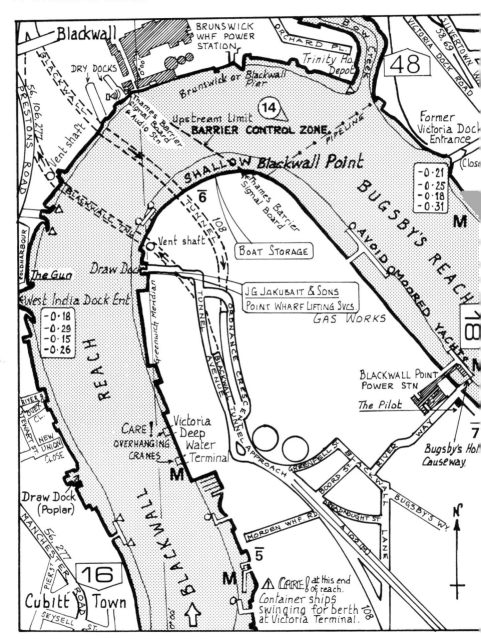

Deptford Creek
The creek is normally only navigable for about 2 hours either side of High Water when an average depth of 8'0" (2.4m) is obtainable. It is not navigable above Deptford Bridge (Blackheath Road). It dries at Low Water. Headroom of Creek Road Bridge at HWS is about 9'0".

Tidal Constants on London Bridge		Mean Tidal Ranges	
HWS — 0 hr 18m		Springs	21'6" 6.56m
LWS — 0 hr 29m	at West India Dock Entrance		
HWN — 0 hr 15m		Neaps	15'0" 4.57m
LWN — 0 hr 26m			

Duration of Rise and Fall of Average Spring and Neap Tides

Flood		Ebb	
Springs	**Neaps**	**Springs**	**Neaps**
5 hrs 45m	6 hrs 30m	6 hrs 30m	6 hrs 00m

Ebb tide sets toward

Reach	*Bank*
Brunswick Wharf	North

Warning: Avoid going too far inshore at Blackwall Point on the south bank as there are shoals here.

CHART DIRECTORY
For key to letter references see p. 21

Port of London Authority
India and Millwall Entrance (01-987 7260)

Lock-keeper's office

J. G. Jakubait & Sons
Point Wharf, Tunnel Avenue, SE10 (01-858 1049)

Marine Engineers
(E, R)

Point Wharf Lifting Services
Point Wharf, Tunnel Avenue, SE10 (01-858 6164)

Marine Engineers
(E)

Boat Storage
Blackwall Point, SE10 (01-854 4155)

Boat store ashore

Victoria Deep Water Terminal Ltd
231, Tunnel Avenue, SE10 (01-858 8161)

Wharfingers

Draw Docks
Poplar
Point Wharf
Bugsby's Hole Causeway, East Greenwich

Samuda Estate
Drawdock Road
River Way, off Blackwall Lane

The Gun *(Inn)*, 27, Cold Harbour, London, E14 (01-987 1692)
The Pilot *(Inn)*, 68, River Way, SE10 (01-858 5910)

For details of Bow Creek see Chart No. 48 on page 158.

Note: All craft intending to negotiate the Thames Barrier should, if fitted with marine VHF R/T, obtain clearance from Barrier Control via Woolwich Radio on Channel 14, when entering the Control Zone at Blackwall Point.

For full instructions see page 82 — 84.

Tidal Constants on London Bridge		Mean Tidal Ranges	
HWS — 0 hr 20m		Springs	21'6"
LWS — 0 hr 35m	at Thames Barrier		6.5m
HWN — 0 hr 20m		Neaps	14'6"
LWN — 0 hr 31m			4.4m

Duration of Rise and Fall of Average Spring and Neap Tides			
Flood		*Ebb*	
Springs	**Neaps**	**Springs**	**Neaps**
5 hrs 45m	6 hrs 40m	6 hrs 25m	5 hrs 45m

Ebb tide sets toward	
Reach	*Bank*
Bugsby's	South. Very strong towards Greenwich YC.
Woolwich	None. Beware of eddies below Barrier.
Gallion's	South. Avoid Gallion's Point.

Light Structure	Characteristics
Margaret Ness (Tripcock Point)	Fl(2)5s 11m

CHART DIRECTORY (Charts 18, 19 and 20)

For key to letter references and symbols see p. 21

Port of London Authority
Thames Barrier Navigation Centre (TBNC),
Hardens Manor Way, Charlton, SE7
(01-855 0315) (VHF Channels 14, 16, 22)

Thames Barrier Control
See separate instructions on
page 82 — 84.

King George V Entrance
Royal Docks, London, E16 (01-476 8774)

Lock-keeper's office

HM Customs
No. 8 Office, Pier Head, King George V Dock,
Royal Docks, London, E16 2PL
(01-476 2231) (VHF Channel 14)

Customs clearance
See Appendix III
(Includes clearance arrange-
ments for St Katharine Haven)

Greenwich Yacht Club
Tideway Sailing Centre, River Way,
East Greenwich, SE10 (01-858 7339)

Sailing Club (ATYC)
(M)

Barrier Gardens Pier
Sargent Brothers (Thames) Ltd, Unity House,
Unity Way, Charlton, SE18
(01-854 5555) (VHF Channel 14)

*Landing in emergency or by
arrangement only.
Passenger trips*
(F)

18 Bugsby's Reach and Thames Barrier

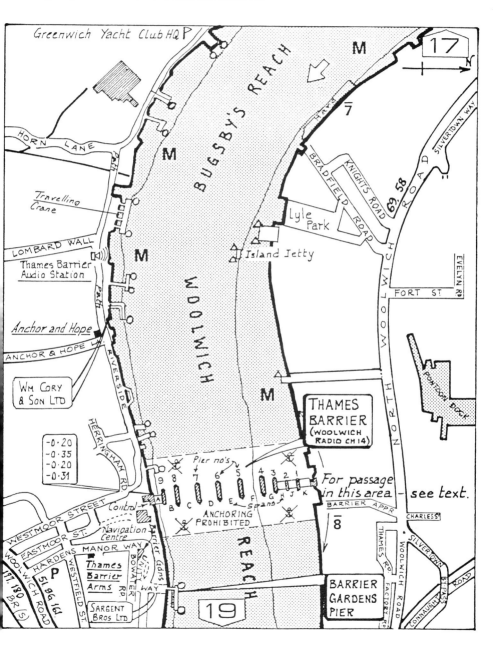

Greenwich Yacht Club HQ

M

17

N

BUGSBY'S REACH

M

7

HORN LANE

Havil

BRADFIELD ROAD

KNIGHTS ROAD

SILVERTOWN WAY

ROAD

69.58

M

Travelling Crane

Lyle Park

WOOLWICH

LOMBARD WALL

Thames Barrier Audio Station

M

Island Jetty

EVELYN RD

FORT ST

Anchor and Hope

ANCHOR & HOPE L

RIVERSIDE

Path

WM CORY & SON LTD

M

THAMES BARRIER
(WOOLWICH RADIO CH 14)

PONTOON DOCK

NORTH

-0·20
-0·35
-0·20
-0·31

HERRINGHAM RD

Pier no's

9 8   7   6   5   4 3 2 1

A

B C D E   F   G H J K

Spans

For passage
in this area — see text.

BARRIER APPR

CHARLES ST

ANCHORING PROHIBITED

8

WESTMOOR STREET

Control

Navigation Centre

Barrier Gdns

THAMES RD

SILVERTOWN

WOOLWICH ROAD

BY PASS

EASTMOOR ST.

MANOR WAY

Thames Barrier Arms

UNITY WAY

BOWATER Rd

19

BARRIER GARDENS PIER

WOOLWICH FACTORY

CONNAUGHT ROAD

P
177 180
BR (S)

WOOLWICH ROAD

51 86 161

WESTFIELD ST.

HARDENS

SARGENT BROS LTD

REACH

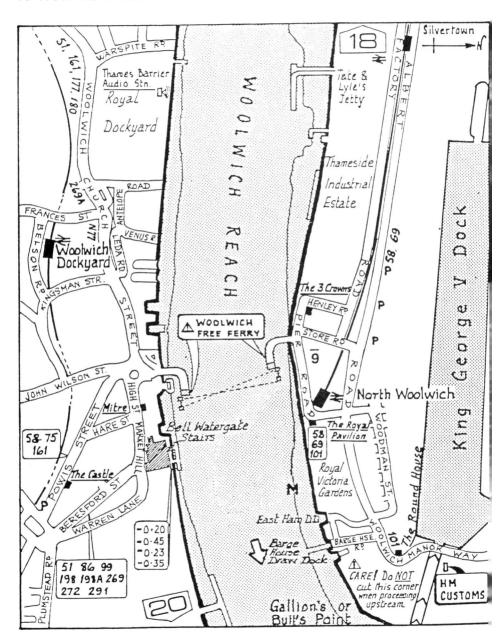

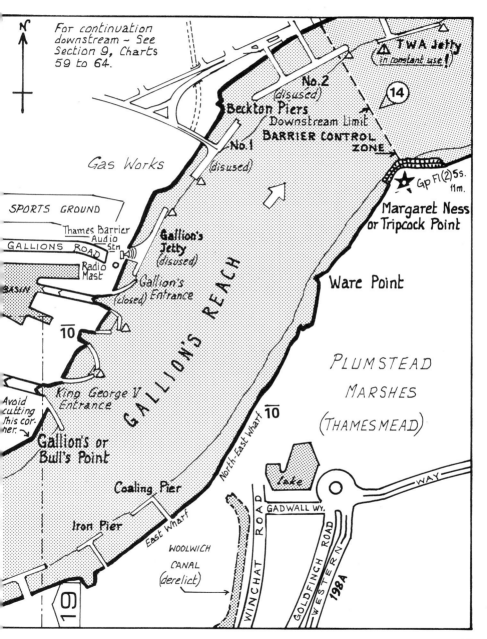

N

For continuation
downstream - See
Section 9, Charts
59 to 64.

TWA Jetty
in constant use!

No.2
(disused)

Beckton Piers
Downstream Limit
BARRIER CONTROL
ZONE

14

No.1
(disused)

Gas Works

Gp Fl(2)5s.
11m.

Margaret Ness
or Tripcock Point

SPORTS GROUND

Thames Barrier
Audio
Stn

GALLIONS ROAD

Gallion's
Jetty
(disused)

Radio
Mast

Gallion's
(closed) Entrance

BASIN

10

Ware Point

GALLION'S REACH

PLUMSTEAD

MARSHES

(THAMESMEAD)

Avoid
cutting
this cor-
ner.

King George V
Entrance

Gallion's or
Bull's Point

10

North-East Wharf

lake

WAY

Coaling Pier

GADWALL WY.

Iron Pier

East Wharf

WOOLWICH

CANAL
(derelict)

WINCHAT ROAD

GOLDFINCH ROAD

WESTERN ROAD

198A

19

Woolwich Free Ferry
High Street, Woolwich SE18 6DX (01-854 3488)

Vehicle ferry

William Cory & Son Ltd
Riverside, Charlton, SE7 7SU (01-858 8181)

Barge and tug owners and lightermen

Thames Barrier Centre
Eastmoor Street, Charlton, SE7 (01-854 1373)

Restaurant and tourist centre

Shore-based fuel supplies

Barrier Gardens Pier (qv) via Hardens Manor Way	**Penby Motors Ltd** 685, Woolwich Road, SE7 (01-858 2144)
Bell Watergate Stairs and Causeway, Woolwich	**Furlongs (Motor Engineers)** 160, Powis Street, SE18 (01-854 3434)
Barge House Causeway, North Woolwich	**K & G Motors** 205, Albert Road, E16 (01-476 3087)

Draw Docks

Bell Watergate Stairs East Ham Draw Dock (not recommended) Barge House Draw Dock	South Bank, off Market Hill North Bank, off Woolwich Manor Way North Bank, off Barge House Road

Anchor and Hope *(Inn),* Riverside, Charlton, SE7 (01-858 0382)
Thames Barrier Arms *(Inn),* 32, Hardens Manor Way, Charlton, SE7 (01-858 7070)
The Three Crowns *(Inn),* 1, Pier Road, North Woolwich, E16 (01-476 1763)
The Mitre *(Inn),* 145, Woolwich High Street, SE18 (01-854 1528/1652)
The Castle *(Hotel),* 179, Powis Street, Woolwich, SE18 (01-854 0259/5118)
The Royal Pavilion *(Inn),* 2, Pier Road, North Woolwich, E16 (01-476 2455)
The Round House *(Inn),* 19, Woolwich Manor Way, E16 (01-476 1320/0932)

THAMES BARRIER

NAVIGATION IN THE THAMES BARRIER CONTROL ZONE

(The Thames Barrier Control Zone extends from Margaret Ness to Blackwall Point).

The Thames Barrier in Woolwich Reach consists of nine piers bedded in the river, numbered from the north bank. The ten spans between the piers are lettered alphabetically from south to north (alpha, etc.). Spans A, H, J and K are permanently closed indicated by three red discs in triangular formation, apex down (replaced with red lights at night or in poor visibility).

Spans B and G, having widths of $103'0''$ (31.5m) and sill depths of $4'0''$ (1.2m) below Chart Datum are suitable for small craft only. Spans C to F inclusive have widths of $200'0''$ (61.0m). Light signals are displayed at the sides of each span from each pier upstream and down, consisting of red crosses and green arrows.

Vessels should, however, only proceed through the spans which have lit green arrows pointing inwards from the adjacent piers. Normally downstream traffic is conducted through spans C and D and upstream traffic through spans E and F. Small craft should use the northernmost or the southernmost span available as signified by the green arrow signals on the piers. NAVIGATION BETWEEN TWO RED CROSSES IS PROHIBITED.

In fog, high intensity white lights will operate in conjunction with the green arrow lights on the ends of Piers 4, 5, 6, 7 and 8.

The barrier is operated by rising sector gates which, when open, lie flat on the bed of the river. The barrier is closed by raising the gates through 90°. Closures in emergency will normally be promulgated by Woolwich Radio (VHF Channel 14) and by a flashing red light operating at the Thames Barrier Signal Stations (large yellow noticeboards) shown on the charts.

In addition to the noticeboards at the Signal Stations there are Audio (loud-hailer) Stations at Brunswick Wharf; half a mile above; and half a mile below the Barrier on the south bank; and at the radar tower below Gallion's Entrance on the north bank. Flashing amber lights at the Signal Stations signify that vessels should proceed with extreme caution. All piers at the Barrier will show lit red crosses.

On seeing a flashing red light at a Barrier Signal Station or noticeboard the master of any vessel should communicate with Thames Barrier Navigation Centre (TBNC) on Channel 14 (VHF). VHF sets should be capable of transmitting and receiving on Channels 14 and 22. If not fitted with VHF radio/telephone the master of such a vessel, on observing a flashing red light at any Signal Station should listen out for messages relayed by loud-hailer at the Audio Stations as shown. Messages originated by Woolwich Radio or by the Morse letter 'K' (—·—) ('I wish to communicate with you') mean that vessels should STOP and contact TBNC by VHF (Channel 14) or wait for further spoken instructions at the Audio Stations if no VHF R/T is fitted to their vessel.

Notes

Overtaking, manoeuvring or use of anchors is not permitted between the Woolwich Ferry Terminal and Island Jetty, except in the event of emergency or with the express permission of TBNC.

Anchoring is prohibited 100 metres either side of the Barrier as shown on Chart 18.

Vessels proceeding under sail only, between the Woolwich Ferry Terminal and Island Jetty, must keep to the starboard side of the fairway and are not to impede other vessels. Wherever possible, vessels should take in their sails and use motor power to navigate through the Barrier.

Routine Barrier Closure for maintenance and testing purposes will be carried out under the Scheme of Operations and prior notice will have been given in the programme published by Thames Water Authority and in PLA Notices to Mariners. Vessels are advised to avoid arranging passage through the Barrier at these times; those which are underway at the time of closure will be directed to designated anchorages.

Large craft (of more than 50 GRT) and all craft regularly transitting the Barrier should request permission to proceed by VHF R/T on Channel 14 (via Woolwich Radio) for each transit at the waypoints shown on the Charts (17 and 20).

Notes compiled from PLA Notice to Mariners No. 12 - 1983 - current at the time of going to press. For the latest information please contact the Assistant Harbour Master's Office at Tower Pier or the Duty Officer at TBNC.

PUBLIC TRANSPORT SERVICES

Railway Services

Station	Region or line	Route	*Normal Frequency
Fenchurch St	ER	South Essex	—
Tower Hill	LT	Circle/District	6/8 mins
Shadwell† **	LT	Metropolitan (East London)	12/20 mins
Wapping†	LT	Metropolitan (East London)	12/20 mins
Rotherhithe†	LT	Metropolitan (East London)	12/20 mins
Stepney (East)	ER	Fenchurch Street — Barking	20 mins
Surrey Docks†	LT	Metropolitan (East London)	12/20 mins
Deptford §	SR	Charing Cross — Woolwich	30 mins
Greenwich §	SR	Charing Cross — Woolwich	30 mins
Silvertown	MR	North Woolwich — Richmond	20 mins
North Woolwich	MR	North Woolwich — Richmond	20 mins
Charlton	SR	Charing Cross — Woolwich	30 mins
Woolwich Dockyard	SR	Charing Cross — Woolwich	30 mins

*Not necessarily on Sundays or at off-peak times. **Closed on Sundays.
†Interchanges with the District/Metropolitan service at Whitechapel.
§Also call at Waterloo (Suburban) and/or start at London Bridge.

London Bus Services

Bus route numbers are shown along principal main roads shown on the charts. Bus route terminals are shown with the route number boxed.

Route No.	Termini	Route No.	Termini
1	Marylebone Station and Catford	51	Orpington and Charlton
1A	Trafalgar Square and Greenwich	53	Camden Town and Plumstead Common
22A	Clapton Park and Wapping Station	54	Woolwich and West Croydon
42	Aldgate and Camberwell Green	56	Aldgate and Poplar
47	Shoreditch and Bromley Common	58	North Woolwich and Walthamstow

69	North Woolwich & Chingford Mount	185	Victoria and Lewisham
70	Surrey Docks & Victoria Station	188	Greenwich Church and Euston Station
75	West Croydon and Woolwich	198	Woolwich and Lower Belvedere
78	Shoreditch and Dulwich	269	Sidcup and Woolwich
86	Romford Station and Limehouse	269A	Bexleyheath and Woolwich
96	Dartford and Woolwich	272	Woolwich and Thamesmead (circ)
99	Woolwich and Slade Green	277	Poplar and Euston
101	North Woolwich and Wanstead	291	Woolwich and Plumstead
106	Finsbury Park and Isle of Dogs	D1	Mile End and Isle of Dogs
108	Stratford and Eltham Church	P5	New Cross and Peckham
108B	Crystal Palace and Surrey Docks		
147	Leytonstone and East Ham	**All-Night Bus Service**	
161	Charlton and Sidcup or Petts Wood	N77	Victoria Station to Thamesmead
177	Woolwich and Waterloo		
180	Abbey Wood and Lower Sydenham Station		

Thames Barrier Signal Station — warning notice, lamps and loud hailers at Brunswick Wharf.

Part II
London's Canals

The Grand Union Canal
Main Line and Paddington Arm

The Regent's Canal

The Hertford Union Canal

The Limehouse Cut

**British
Waterways
Board**

MAXIMUM DIMENSIONS OF CRAFT ON LONDON'S CANALS

Regent's and Grand Union Canals*

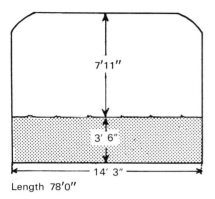

Length 78'0"

Lee Navigation and Hertford Union Canal

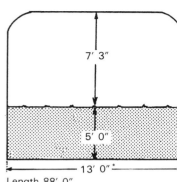

Length 88' 0"
Length - Hertford Union 84' 0"
*Below Enfield 18' 0"

Maida Hill Tunnel

Islington Tunnel

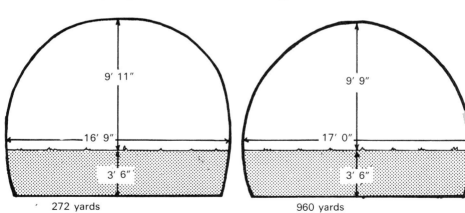

272 yards   960 yards

The above diagrams do not represent true profiles of the bridges, tunnels and locks referred to but represent graphically the maximum dimensions of craft which will pass such structures.

*For slight variations, consult the individual section introductions which quote precise figures for that section only. The above is only given as a general guide.

BRITISH WATERWAYS BOARD TELEPHONE DIRECTORY

Useful numbers for boat-owners and others making use of this pilot.

Headquarters, Melbury House	01-262 6711
Area Leisure Officer (London)	Watford (0923) 31363
Paddington Inquiry Office and Shop	01-286 6101 / 01-289 9897
Regents Canal Information Centre, Camden Locks	01-482 0523
Engineering Area, Section and Yard and Lock numbers	
London Area Engineer	Watford (0923) 31363
Brentford Section (Grand Union)	01-574 1220
Lee Section (Lee Navigation)	Lea Valley (0992) 764626
Regent's Section (Regent's Canal)	01-790 3444
Locks	
Bow Locks	01-987 5661
Brentford Gauging Locks	01-560 1120
Brentford Gauging Locks (after normal wkg hours)	01-560 8942
Enfield Lock	Lea Valley (0992) 768230
Hanwell (No. 97) Lock	01-567 4867
Hampstead Road Lock	01-485 2923
Hertford Union Lock (Upper)	01-980 1946
Limehouse Ship Lock	01-790 3444
Norwood Top	01-574 0131
Old Ford (Regent's) Lock	01-980 1426
Old Ford (Lee) Locks	01-985 4162
Picketts Lock	01-807 4650
Ponders End Lock	01-804 1303
Rammey Marsh Lock	Lea Valley (0992) 762831
Salmon's Lane Lock	01-987 1963
Stonebridge Lock	01-808 4643
Thames Locks (Brentford)	01-560 2779/8943
Tottenham Locks	01-808 3918
Weirs	
Lea Bridge	01-985 4876
Newman's, Enfield	Lea Valley (0992) 762548
Foremen and Lengthmen	
Regent's Section *(out of hours)*	Lea Valley (0992) 764626
North Circular Road Aqueduct	01-965 5606
Lower Lee	01-805 2151
Lee Navigation *(out of hours)*	Lea Valley (0992) 764626
Yards and Workshops	
Bull's Bridge	01-573 2368
Enfield Depot *(Freight)*	01-804 5552
Enfield Maintenance Yard	Lea Valley (0992) 764626
Brentford Depot	01-560 8941
Canalphone *Recorded Message Service (South)*	01-723 8487
Security Force *(Towpath patrols, etc.)*	01-987 1321
Craft Licensing Office	Watford (0923) 26422

STD codes If dialling from outside London include 01- where shown. Outside London for Lea Valley dial 0992- and for Watford dial 0923-. If calling Lea Valley or Watford from within the London Area on a telephone showing an '01' number consult the Code Instruction booklet.

KEY TO CANAL CHARTS

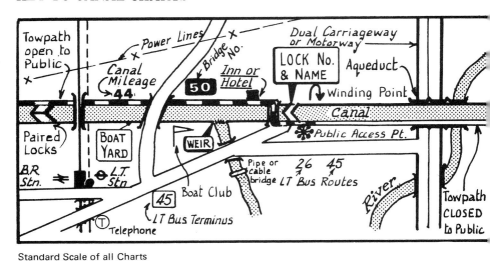

Standard Scale of all Charts

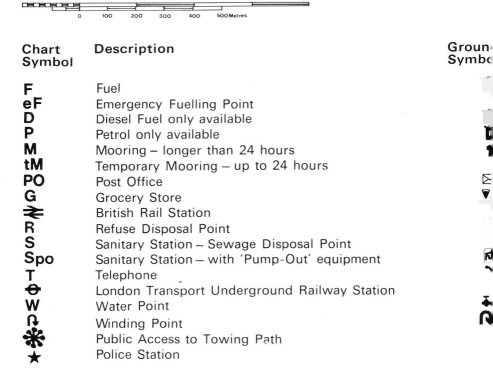

Chart Symbol	Description	Groun Symbo
F	Fuel	
eF	Emergency Fuelling Point	
D	Diesel Fuel only available	
P	Petrol only available	
M	Mooring – longer than 24 hours	
tM	Temporary Mooring – up to 24 hours	
PO	Post Office	
G	Grocery Store	
⇌	British Rail Station	
R	Refuse Disposal Point	
S	Sanitary Station – Sewage Disposal Point	
Spo	Sanitary Station – with 'Pump-Out' equipment	
T	Telephone	
⊖	London Transport Underground Railway Station	
W	Water Point	
↻	Winding Point	
❋	Public Access to Towing Path	
★	Police Station	

Section 5 Grand Union Canal – Main Line Brentford to Harefield

Distance	17 statute land miles
Number of Locks	19
Tunnels	None
Bridges	47 (not including access bridges at paired locks)
Branches	River Brent – Maypole Dock – Adelaide Dock – Paddington Arm (comprising Section 6 of this pilot) – Slough Arm (5 miles) (not charted but see p. 104 for directory) – Widewater – Troy Cut. Cruising Waterway (Transport Act, 1968)
Status	Cruising Waterway (Transport Act, 1968)

Maximum dimensions of craft:

Headroom	7'11"
Length	78'0"
Beam	14'3"
Draught	3'6"

Waterway Authority (for navigation)

British Waterways Board
Melbury House, Melbury Terrace, London, NW1 6JX (01-262 6711).
London Area Engineer
British Waterways Board
43 Clarendon Road, Watford, Hertfordshire, WD1 1JE (Watford (0923) 31363).
Brentford Section Inspector
British Waterways Board
Norwood Top Lock, Southall, Middx (01-574 1220).

Licensing:

All craft proceeding on this and the waterways in Sections 6, 7 and 8 must have a valid craft licence, obtainable on application to:

The Craft Licensing Supervisor
British Waterways Board, Willow Grange, Church Road, Watford, Hertfordshire WD1 3QA (Watford (0923) 26422).

Licences are issued on receipt of suitable application details on the prescribed form together with the appropriate remittance for periods of 1 month, 3 months, 6 months or 1 year. Annual licences normally run from April 1st in any year. Licence plates issued must, to conform to BWB bye-laws, be fixed in a conspicuous position on the vessel to facilitate inspection.

Office and lock telephone numbers appear in the text where appropriate. An alphabetical directory of BWB telephone numbers appears for easy reference on page 89.

SPEED LIMIT ON ALL SECTIONS – 4 mph

ENTRY TO GRAND UNION CANAL (MAIN LINE) AT BRENTFORD

Entry to the Grand Union is made by turning into Brentford Creek from the River Thames on the Middlesex Bank about 1½ miles below Richmond. From upstream the entrance is inconspicuous but lies just below Syon Park and Brentford Dock Marina against which there used to be numerous barge moorings. A PLA Driftwood barge is moored upstream of the marina and canal entrances in the Thames.

Thames Lock (No. 101) is the first lock and is paired, being worked on weekdays, except Bank Holidays, from two hours before High Water in Brentford Creek until two hours after, within the period 0600 hours to 2200 hours.

Brentford Lock (No. 100) is the next lock and is only part tidal, being open on weekdays all day from 0700 hours to 1800 hours. On Saturdays and Sundays, and on selected Bank Holidays in the summer season within the period 0600 to 2200 both locks are worked only from two hours before High Water to two hours after. However if the times of High Water mean that the working period would be less than one hour no staff will be in attendance for passing craft through the locks and passage will not therefore be possible.

Working of these locks by boat crews is prohibited.

All locks are designed to pass craft of maximum dimensions 72'0" long, 14'3" wide, drawing 3'6". The actual depth quoted by some authorities may exceed this figure but one has to make allowances for silting.

If planning to enter or leave these locks, it is strongly recommended that skippers telephone the lock-keeper well in advance on 01-560 1120 from Teddington, Southall or from the point of departure downstream on the River Thames.

On high tides (Springs) you should note that the headroom of Dock Road Bridge which crosses the tail of Thames Locks, which are tidal, can be as little as 7'0". You may therefore have to be prepared to wait outside the lock in the creek until the tide has fallen sufficiently for your vessel to clear the bridge. The spring tidal range at this point is approximately 17 feet. Since the pound above Thames Locks is part tidal the headroom under Brentford High Street Bridge (No. 209) may also be restricted.

Details of how to calculate the tides and times of entry into the canal are contained in the preamble to Section 1 of this guide.

METHOD

If you arrive off the creek when the tidal locks are closed it is advisable to moor in the Thames against the opposite (Surrey) bank. Mooring should be effected by means of anchors, clear of the fairway but sufficiently away from the bank to prevent grounding on a low tide. On the middlesex bank, barge traffic may be encountered and there are a number of barge moorings in the river at Brentford, particularly downstream of the creek entrance.

You are well advised to notify the lock-keeper at Brentford of your ETA by telephone (as above). The lock-keeper will then advise you as to the best time to enter the creek. You will be directed as to which of the tidal locks you should enter when you arrive. If not so directed, approach the chamber which is open to you, or if no lock is ready, hold off in the creek until the lock is ready. A lighted signal in the form of an arrow indicates the chamber to be used. Thames Locks are paired and are mechanically operated from a cabin on the lock island. Having entered the lock, make fast quickly and watch the sluice indicators on the white square posts at the ends of each lock. Boat owners are prohibited from attempting to operate these locks for themselves.

Leaving Thames Locks, the canal winds past old warehouses and a new development of blocks of flats on the port hand. Note that between Thames and Brentford Locks there is no towing path but footpaths exist close to the canal and these are shown in the detail chart for Brentford on p.   . Passing beneath the new footbridge after the bottom weir, the canal turns to port and then to starboard to Brentford High Street Bridge. This latter bridge has a curved soffit arch and should be approached with caution in view of the proximity of Brentford Gauging Locks on the far side. Before negotiating the bridge, which should be passed as close to the centre of the arch as possible, make certain that it is clear to do so and that the Gauging Locks can be entered or that a reasonable mooring can be made on the port hand just below the locks.

There may be lighter traffic on this section and a careful lookout should be maintained, your cruiser being navigated at minimum speed to give adequate steerage way. Brentford Gauging Locks (No. 100) are also paired. The lock-keeper will signal which chamber should be entered. Note that mooring lines should be fastened to the power winches by means of one turn only, so that the cruiser can be winched steady by the lock-keeper. Lock-men in attendance, if any, will then secure them by means of a 'tugboat' hitch.

The sluices and gates are also mechanically operated, so be prepared to adjust the trim of your craft by leaving the engine running and engaging gear if necessary.

The towing path starts on the left-hand* bank and continues as a public path as shown on the charts. Once clear of Brentford and the commercial wharves and traffic the canal narrows and becomes countrified, apart from the odd sightings of the M4 Motorway, as far as the Hanwell Flight and Southall.

The first self-operated lock is New Brentford or Clitheroe's (No. 99) and is now provided with a new type of easy winding sluice gear. Arrows on the winding gear casing show the direction to turn to open or close the sluices — *up* for *open* and *down* for *shut*. Pointers are also provided on the heads of the sluice control shafts on the gates indicating whether the sluices are open or shut. Further locks up the canal are also provided with this new pattern mechanism.

*In deference to normal canal parlance, now that we have left the river, we shall be using the terms *left* and *right* hand in lieu of *port* and *starboard*. Thus, *left* is always the left-hand side of your ship as viewed from the stern and *right* the right-hand side.

In designating the bank of a canal, the normal practice is to refer to the *towpath* side — that side on which the towing-path is, or was, laid; and the *off* side — that side opposite the *towpath* side. It will be appreciated that this is not always the same side throughout the canal.

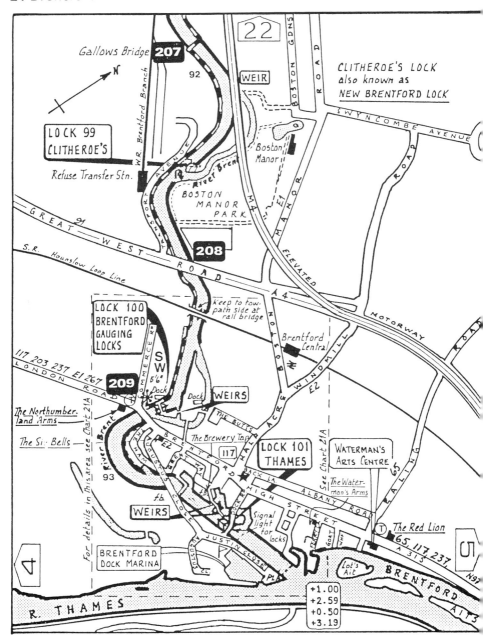

Tidal Constants on London Bridge		Mean Tidal Ranges	
HWS + 1 hr 00m	⎫	Springs	17'0"
LWS + 2 hr 59m	⎬ at Thames Locks	*Below locks*	5.18m
HWN + 0 hr 50m	⎬	Neaps	13'0"
LWN + 3 hr 19m	⎭	*Below locks*	3.96m

Duration of Rise and Fall of Average Spring and Neap Tides

Flood		*Ebb*	
Springs	**Neaps**	**Springs**	**Neaps**
3 hrs 45m	4 hrs 00m	8 hrs 45m	8 hrs 45m

Ebb tide sets toward

Reach	*Bank*
Above Brentford Creek	Surrey
Below Brentford Creek	Middlesex

Licensing

If you have not previously licensed your craft to navigate on British Waterways Board waterways, you may complete the necessary formalities at the Brentford Depot Office at Brentford Gauging Locks, during normal business hours (0800–1700) Monday to Friday.

Lock rise (or fall)	Lock Name and No.	Falls from	Rises from
Tidal (Mechanical)	Thames (101) (Paired)	Cowroast	R. Thames
5'6" (Mechanical) (Pt tidal)	Brentford (100) (Paired)	Cowroast	R. Thames
Locks only worked by keepers.			
7'7" (Hand) Lock worked by boat crews	Clitheroe's (99)	Cowroast	R. Thames

CHART DIRECTORY

For key to letter references see p. 21
For method of entry and departure at Thames Locks see pages 92 and 93

Thames Locks (No. 101)
Dock Road, Brentford, Middx
(01-568 2779)

British Waterways Board Lock.
(Out of working hours call
01-568 2779 or 01-560 8943).
Locks only worked by keeper.

Brentford Gauging Locks (No. 100)
High Street, Brentford, Middx
(01-560 1120)

British Waterways Board Lock.
(Out of working hours call
01-560 8942)
tM, S, U, W
Locks only worked by keeper.

Brentford Dock Marina
Justin Close, Brentford, Middx TW8 8QQ
(01-568 0287)

Marina & Club
See page 36 for full details

E. C. Jones & Son (Brentford) Ltd (01-560 7494)
E. G. Harris Ltd (01-568 6893)
Brentside Wharf, Dock Road, Brentford, Middx
TW8 8AQ

Boat builders & marine engineers
Waterscape contractors

Brentford Yacht and Boat Co. Ltd
Brent Way, Brentford, Middx. (01-560 6561)

Moorings and fuel in emergency.
(eD, eP, M)

Brentford Bridge Boat Yard
Durham Wharf, High St, Brentford, Middx
(01-847 1538)

Boat & Engine repairs

G. T. Steel Craft Ltd
Brent Wharf, High Street, Brentford, Middx TW8 8JY
(01-568 1123)

Boat builders

Metropolitan Police
Half Acre, Brentford, Middx (01-577 1212)

Emergency calls only – Dial 999

The Waterman's Arts Centre, 40 High Street, Brentford, Middx (01-568 1176 (Bookings)
The Brewery Tap *(Inn),* 17 Catherine Wheel Road, Brentford, Middx (01-560 5200)
The Northumberland Arms *(Inn),* 11 London Road, Brentford, Middx (01-560 1119/0506)
The Red Lion *(Inn),* High Street, Brentford, Middx (01-560 6181)
The Six Bells *(Inn),* High Street, Brentford, Middx (01-560 8804)
The Waterman's Arms *(Inn),* 1 Ferry Lane, Brentford, Middx (01-568 5665)

a Brentford (detail)

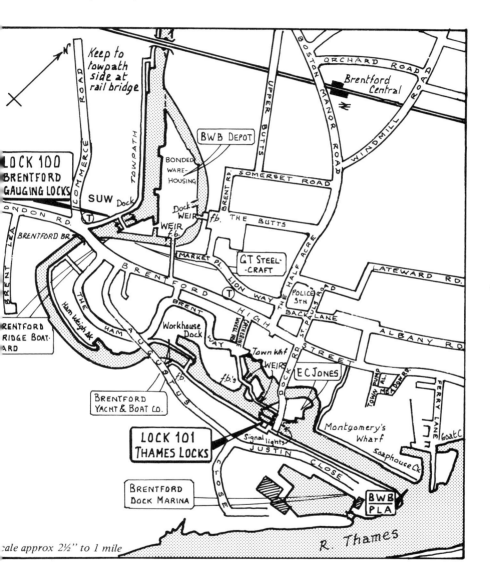

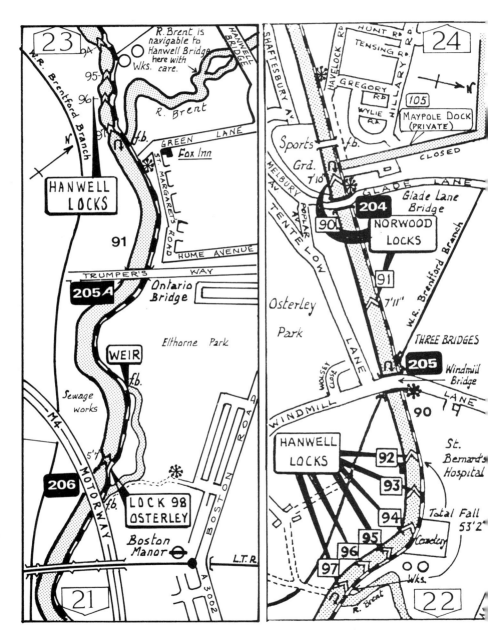

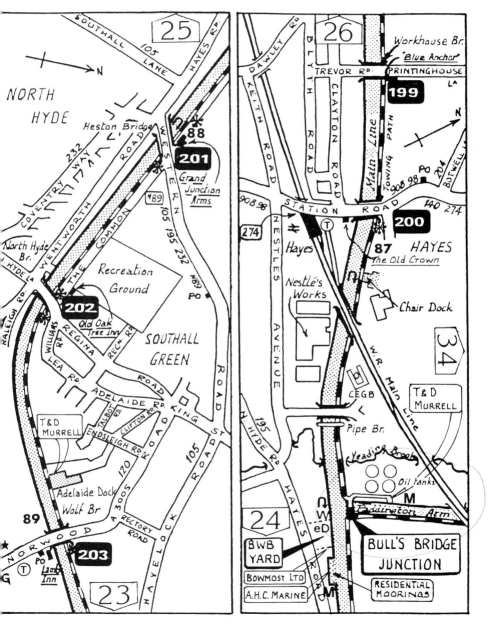

Lock rise (or fall)		Lock Name and No.	Falls from	Rises from
5'7"		Osterley (98)	Cowroast	R. Thames
8'11"		Hanwell Bottom (97)	Cowroast	R. Thames
8'11"	All locks	Hanwell Flight (96)	Cowroast	R. Thames
8'10"		Hanwell Flight (95)	Cowroast	R. Thames
8'10"	worked by	Hanwell Flight (94) (Asylum)	Cowroast	R. Thames
8'10"		Hanwell Flight (93)	Cowroast	R. Thames
8'10"	boat crew	Hanwell Top (92)	Cowroast	R. Thames
7'11"		Norwood Bottom (91)	Cowroast	R. Thames
7'10"		Norwood Top (90)	Cowroast	R. Thames

For safety reasons Locks 90 and 97 are padlocked between 20.30 and 08.00 nightly.

CHART DIRECTORY (Charts 22 – 25)

For key to letter references see p. 21

22, 23 **Hanwell Bottom Lock**
Green Lane, Hanwell, London, W7

British Waterways Board Lock.
(M) Overnight, below lock.

23 **Brentford Section Engineer**
Norwood Top Lock, Southall, Middx
(01-574 1220)

British Waterways Board Section Engineer.
(S, U, W)

25 **Bull's Bridge Yard**
Bull's Bridge Junction, Hayes Road,
Southall, Middx (01-573 2368)

British Waterways Board Maintenance and Repair Yard.
(D, W) Emergency supplies only.

24 **T & D Murrell (Adelaide Dock Co)**
Adelaide Dock, Endsleigh Rd, Southall
UB2 5QR (01-571 5678)

Boatyard, barge owners & carriers
(B, C, E, F, R)

24 **Colne Valley Passenger Boats**
Adelaide Dock, Endsleigh Rd, Southall
UB2 5QR (01-571 4428)

Passenger Vessel Operators.
(F)

25 **AHC Marine**
Willow Wren Wharf, Hayes Road,
Southall (01-573 2008)

Chandlers

25 **Bowmost Limited**
36, Canal Yard, Hayes Road, Southall,
Middx (01-571 2037)

Boatbuilders & repairers

24 **Metropolitan Police**
Norwood Green Station, 190 Norwood
Road, Southall, Middx (01-900 7212)

Emergency calls only – Dial 999

22 The Fox Inn, Green Lane, Hanwell, London, W7 (01-567 3912)
24 The Lamb Inn, Norwood Road, Southall, Middx (01-574 5555)
24 The Old Oak Tree *(Inn)*, The Common, Southall, Middx (01-574 1714)
24 The Grand Junction Arms *(Inn)*, The Common, Western Road, Southall, Middx (01-574 3350)
25 The Old Crown *(Inn)*, Station Road, Hayes, Middx (01-573 7141)
25 The Blue Anchor *(Inn)*, Printing House Lane, Hayes, Middx (01-573 0714)

Towpath Access Points: Boston Manor Park, below Osterley Lock; Ontario Bridge; Green Lane, Hanwell; Windmill Bridge; Glade Lane Bridge; Havelock Road; Wolf Bridge; North Hyde Bridge; Heston Bridge; Station Road, Hayes.

Lock rise (or fall)	Lock Name and No.	Falls from	Rises from
6'6"	Cowley (89)	Cowroast	R. Thames
4'7"	Uxbridge (88)	Cowroast	R. Thames

All locks worked by boat crews.

CHART DIRECTORY (Charts 26 – 29)

For key to letter references see p. 21

28   **High Line Yachting Ltd**
     Packet Boat Lane, Cowley Peachey, Middx
     (West Drayton (0895) 442290)
     Boatyard
     (D, G, Spo, U, W)
     Mooring

28   **Technical Marine Services**
     my *White Aster*, Benbow Way, Cowley,
     Uxbridge, Middx (Uxbridge (0895) 52021)
     Marine Engineers

28   **†Cowley Lock**
     Iver Lane, Cowley, Middx
     British Waterways Board Lock and
     Moorings.
     (M, S, W)

29   **Marine Engine Services**
     Uxbridge Wharf, 23a Waterloo Road,
     Uxbridge, Middx (Uxbridge (0895) 70422)

29   **Uxbridge Boat Centre Ltd**
     23 Waterloo Road, Uxbridge, Middx
     (Uxbridge (0895) 52019)
     Boatyard
     (C, D, G, I, M, P, U, W, R, B, etc.)
     Uxbridge Cruising Club base.

29   **Denham Marina Ltd**
     Denham Yacht Station
     100 Acres, Uxbridge, Middx
     (Uxbridge (0895) 39811)
     Boatyard & Marina
     (C, D, G, H, M, P, R, S, U, W)
     Denham Cruising Club base.

27   **Metropolitan Police**
     Station Road, West Drayton, Middx
     (01-897 7373)
     Emergency calls only – Dial 999

29   **Metropolitan Police**
     49 Windsor Street, Uxbridge, Middx
     (01-900 7212)
     Emergency calls only – Dial 999

26   **The Woolpack** *(Inn)*, Dawley Road, Hayes, Middx (01-573 2998)
26   **The Foresters** *(Inn)*, Chapel Lane, West Drayton (West Drayton (08954) 43535)
27   **The De Burgh Arms** *(Inn)*, High Street, West Drayton, Middx (WD (08954) 42018)
27   **The Anchor** *(Inn)*, 39 High Street, Yiewsley, Middx (WD (08954) 42764)
28   **S J's Wine Bar**, Packet Boat Lane, Cowley Peachey, Uxbridge (WD (08954) 41596)

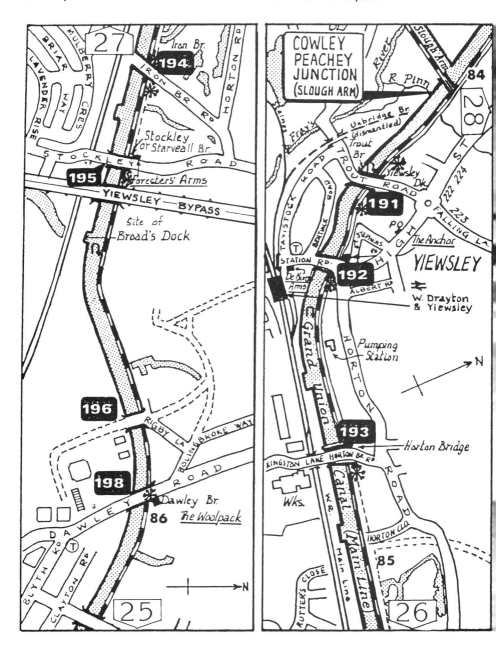

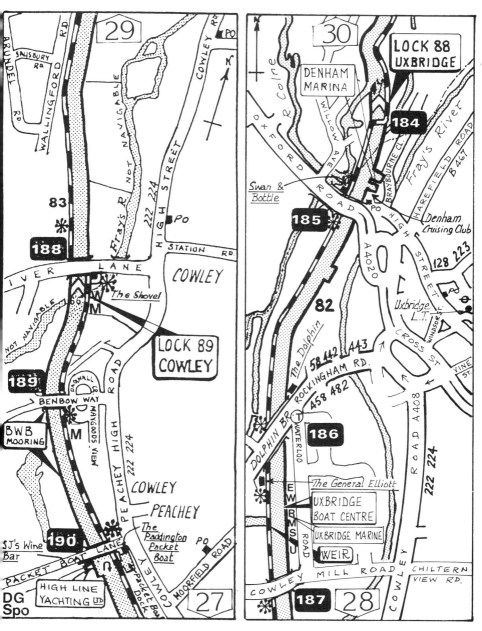

28   The Paddington Packet Boat *(Inn)*, Cowley Peachey High Rd (WD (08954) 42392)
28   The Shovel *(Inn)*, Cowley Lock, Iver Lane, Cowley, Middx (Uxbridge (0895) 33121)
29   The General Elliott *(Inn)*, St John's Road, Uxbridge (Uxbridge (0895) 37385)
29   The Dolphin *(Inn)*, Rockingham Road, Uxbridge (Uxbridge (0895) 32656)
29   The Swan and Bottle *(Restaurant)*, 98 Oxford Road, Uxbridge (Uxbridge (0895) 34047)

†British Waterways Board Moorings:
28   'Special' Class site – Benbow Waye (Outer London and Provinces)   Category 1
28   'A' Class site – Cowley Lock   Category A

Towpath Access Points: Dawley Bridge (The Woolpack); Stockley Road (Starveall Bridge); Iron Bridge; Horton Bridge; Station Road, West Drayton; Trout Bridge; Packet Boat Lane; Benbow Bridge; Iver Lane (both sides); Cowley Mill Road; Dolphin Bridge, Uxbridge (both sides); Oxford Road Bridge, Uxbridge (both sides); off Western Avenue (A40); Denham Lock; Bridge 182; Moorhall Road, Harefield; Broadwater Lane; Black Jack's Bridge (178); Coppermill Bridge; Springwell Bridge.

Slough Arm (not charted)

(27)   **High Line Yachting Ltd**   *Boatyard and Cruiser Hire*
         The Boatyard, Mansion Lane, Iver,   (B, C, D, G, H, M, R, S, U, W)
         Bucks SL0 9RE (Iver (0753) 651496)

Lock rise (or fall)	Lock Name and No.	Falls from	Rises from
4'7"	Uxbridge (88)	Cowroast	R. Thames
11'1"	Denham (87)	Cowroast	R. Thames
8'0"	Harefield (86) (Widewater)	Cowroast	R. Thames
3'8"	Black Jack's (85)	Cowroast	R. Thames
5'10"	Copper Mill (84)	Cowroast	R. Thames
7'11"	Springwell (83)	Cowroast	R. Thames

All locks unattended and worked by boat crews.

CHART DIRECTORY (Charts 30 – 33)
For key to letter references see p. 21

         British Waterways Board   *Emergency Only*
         Grand Union Canal, Apsley Section Foreman,
         (Residence) (Harefield (089 582) 3509)

31   **Harefield Boatyard**   *Boatyard*
         Moor Hall Road, Harefield, Middx   (M)

31   **The Horse and Barge** *(Inn)*, Moor Hall Road, Denham, Bucks (Denham (0895) 832189/834080)
         The Fisheries Inn, Copper Mill, Harefield, Middx (Harefield (089 582) 3180/2532)

30 Denham

31 Harefield Moor

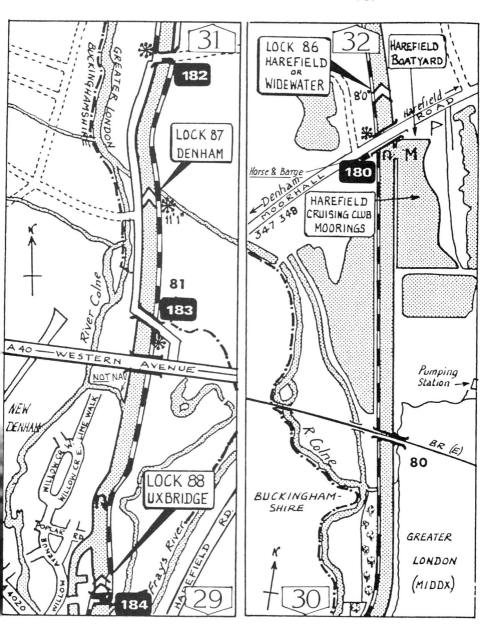

32 Harefield

33 Springwell

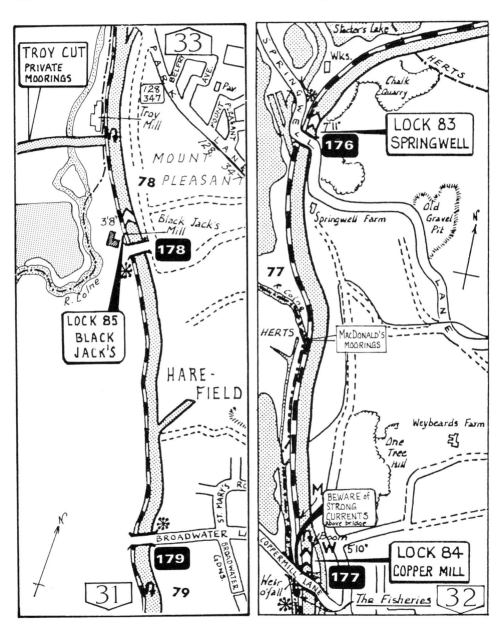

For continuation north – See the OS Nicholson's *Guide to the Waterways Volume 1 – South* or *Waterways World Guide to Grand Union Canal (South).*

PUBLIC TRANSPORT SERVICES

Railway Services

Station	Region or line	Route	*Normal Frequency
Brentford Central	SR	Waterloo – Hounslow	30 mins
Boston Manor	LT	Piccadilly (Heathrow)	12 mins
Hayes & Harlington	WR	Paddington – Slough	30 mins
West Drayton & Yiewsley	WR	Paddington–Slough	30 mins
Southall	WR	Paddington–Slough	30 mins
Uxbridge	LT	Metropolitan/Piccadilly	12/15 mins

Not necessarily on Sundays or at 'off-peak' times.

London Bus Services

Bus route numbers are shown along principal main roads shown on the charts. Bus route terminals are shown with the route number boxed, except at Uxbridge LT Station where the details are given below.

Uxbridge LT, (Underground) Station Bus Terminus
Routes 98, 128, 204, 207, 222, 224, N89, London Country 58, 305, 325, 347, 348, 442, 443, 458, 482.

Route No.	Termini	Route No.	Termini
65	Chessington Zoo and Ealing Broadway	207	Uxbridge and Shepherds Bush
90B	Kew Gardens Station and Yeading	222	Hounslow and Uxbridge Station
91	Wandsworth and Hounslow West	223	Ruislip Station and Heathrow Airport Central
98	Hounslow and Uxbridge Station	224	Uxbridge Station and Stockley
105	Shepherds Bush and Heathrow Airport Central	232	Hounslow and Yeading
117	Brentford and Staines	237	Shepherds Bush and Sunbury Village
120	Hounslow Heath and Greenford	267	Hampton Court Station and Hammersmith
128	Local service between Harefield, Rickmansworth, Ruislip and Uxbridge	274	Ealing Broadway Station and Hayes Station
195	Charville Lane Estate and Southfield (Ealing Hosp.)		Flat Fare routes *(Pay as you enter)*
203	Brentford and Staines	E1	Greenford and Brentford
204	Uxbridge and Hayes	E2	Ruislip and Brentford

London Country Bus Routes

305	High Wycombe and Uxbridge	442	Uxbridge and Staines or Thorpe Park
325	Luton and Uxbridge	443	Uxbridge and Staines
347	Hemel Hempstead and Uxbridge	458	Uxbridge and Windsor
348	Hemel Hempstead and Uxbridge	482	Uxbridge and Windsor

Taylor Woodrow's offices spanning the Paddington Arm of the Grand Union Canal at Yeading

Section 6 Grand Union Canal Paddington Arm

Distance	13 statute land miles (to Junction with Regent's Canal)
Number of Locks	None
Tunnels	None
Bridges	42 (including 3 over branch to Paddington Basin)
Branches	*Lyon's Dock; *Kensal Gas Works Docks (2); St Anne's (now Port A Bella) Dock; Paddington Basin (6 furlong extension from Junction with Regent's Canal). *Although these docks are still in existence the entrances are barred at water level.*
Status	As Section 5

Maximum dimensions of craft:

Headroom	7'11"
Length	78'0"
Beam	14'3"
Draught	3'6"

Waterway Authority (for navigation) For details see preamble to Section 5

Brentford Section Engineer
    British Waterways Board, Norwood Top Lock, Southall, Middx (01-574 1220).
Information and Sales Office
    British Waterways Board, Canal Office, Delamere Terrace, Paddington, London, W2 6ND (01-286 6101/01-289 9897).

Licensing See preamble to Section 5

SPEED LIMIT THROUGHOUT – 4 mph

NAVIGATION NOTES

There are no locks on this section which lies mainly through industrial and residential areas, west of London. However, the scenery is enhanced by rural stretches past Horsenden Hill and several recreation areas. A highlight is the crossing of the North Circular Road, near Alperton, by means of an aqueduct – viewed by most motorists, not in the know, as another railway bridge.

    The final approach to Little Venice is probably one of the most picturesque in the southeast. Passing the Paddington Toll Office, now used as a shop and information centre, the Paddington Arm turns southeast under the Harrow Road towards Paddington Basin. The main channel is now deemed to continue northeast, leaving Browning's Island on the right hand. There is no need to approach the Regent's Canal by circuiting the island, the waterbuses moor and manoeuvre on the south side and the passage may be obstructed.

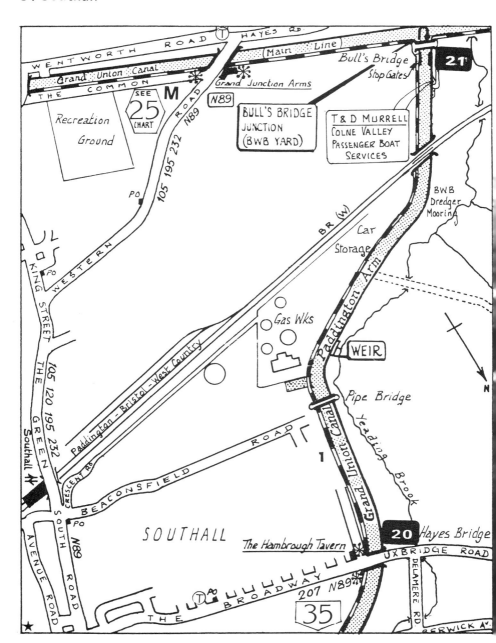

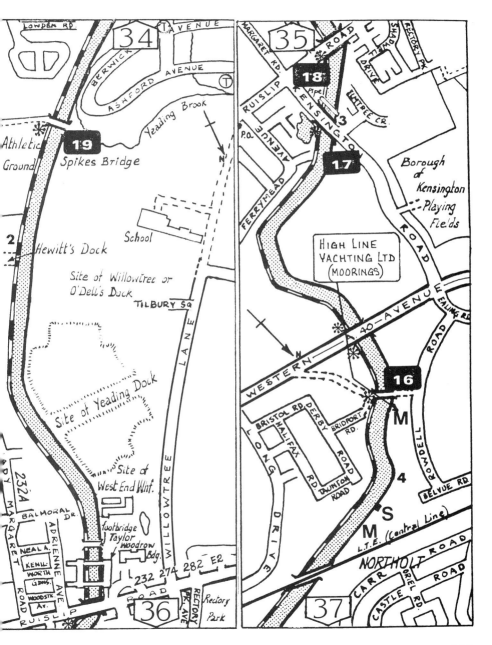

37 Greenford

38 Alperton

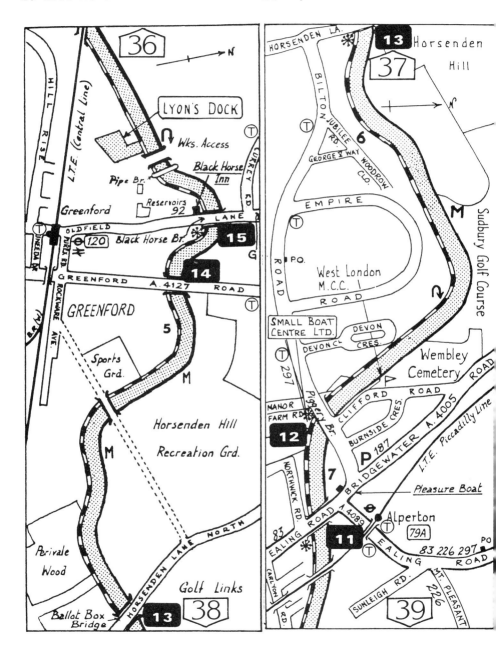

CHART DIRECTORY (Charts 34 – 38)
For key to letter references see p. 21

34	**Bull's Bridge Yard** Bull's Bridge Junction, Hayes Road, Southall, Middx (01-573 2368)	*British Waterways Board* *Maintenance and Repair Yard* (D, W) Emergency supplies only
34	**Colne Valley Passenger Boat Services** The Toll House, Bull's Bridge Wharf, Southall, Middx (01-848 4485)	*Passenger trips* (F)
34	**Metropolitan Police** 67 High Street, Southall, Middx (01-900 7212)	*Emergency calls only – Dial 999*
36	**High Line Yachting Ltd** Rowdell Road, Northolt, Middx (01-845 9924) *(For main office, see page 104)*	*Mooring and storage* (M, S, T, U, W) (C, D, G)
37	**Metropolitan Police** 21 Oldfield Lane, Greenford, Middx (01-900 7212)	*Emergency calls only – Dial 999*
38	**Small Boat Centre Ltd** Piggery Wharf, Manor Farm Rd, Wembley, Middx (01-997 7496)	*Boatbuilders & Repairers*
38	**West London Motor Cruising Club** (Secretary, 146 Sandy Lane, Cheam, Surrey)	*Cruising Club* (M) (Based at Alperton)
38	**Chain Garages (Alperton) Ltd** Bridgewater Road, Alperton, Middx (01-902 5354/5460)	*Fuel (not canalside)* (P)

34	**The Hambrough Tavern** *(Inn)*, Uxbridge Road, Southall (01-574 8295)
34	**The Grand Junction Arms** *(Inn)*, The Common, Southall, Middx (01-574 3350)
37	**The Black Horse** *(Inn)*, Black Horse Bridge, 425 Oldfield Lane, Greenford, Middx (01-578 1384)
37	**The Ballot Box Inn**, Horsenden Lane North, Greenford (01-902 2825)
38	**The Pleasure Boat** *(Inn)*, 346 Ealing Road, Wembley, Middx (01-902 4516)

Towing Path Access Points: Hayes Bridge (No. 20), Uxbridge Road; Spikes Bridge (No. 19); Ruislip Road (No. 18); Kensington Road (No. 17); Western Avenue (A 40) Bridge; Bridport Road (No. 16); Black Horse Bridge (No. 15); Ballot Box Bridge (No. 13); Piggery Bridge (No. 12); Ealing Road (No. 11)

Overnight Moorings
Good overnight moorings may be had on the off-side below Horsenden Hill
Recreation Grounds and Sudbury Golf Course.

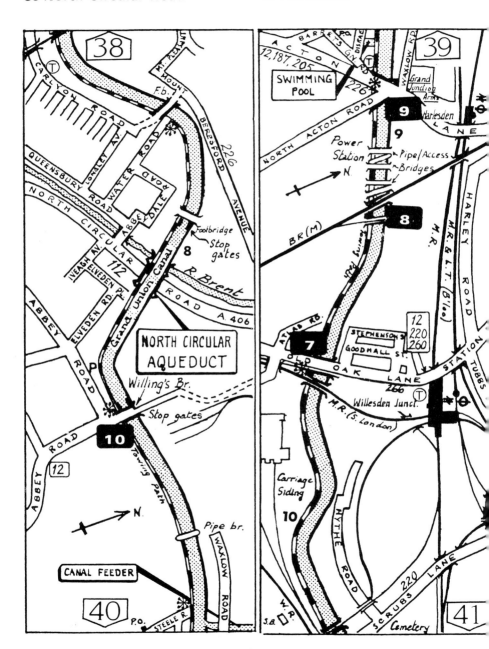

1 Kensal Green

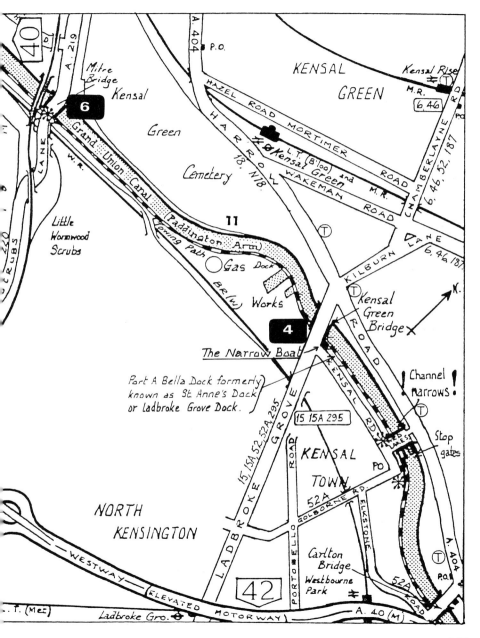

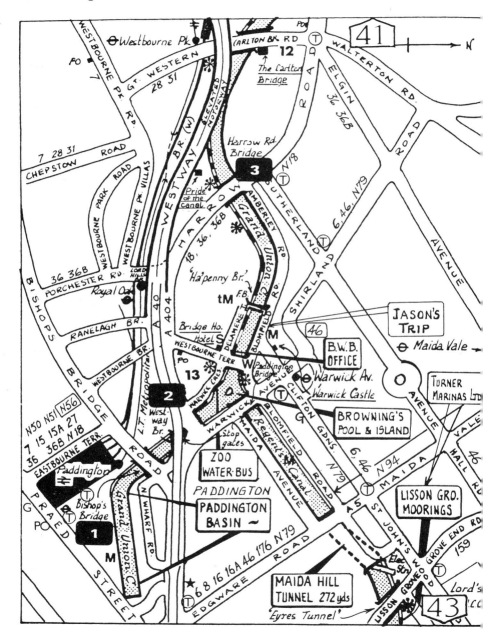

Grand Union Canal and the Westway   Photo: *Derek Pratt*

CHART DIRECTORY (Charts 39–42)
For key to letter references see p. 21

39	**British Waterways Board** Lengthsman's Cottage, North Circular Aqueduct (01-965 5606)	*Aqueduct Maintenance*
39	**Twyford Service Station Ltd** Twyford Abbey Road, London, NW10 (01-965 6494)	*Canalside Fuel* *(Petrol & Autodiesel)*
40	**Metropolitan Police** 75 Craven Park, Harlesden, NW10 (01-900 7212)	*Emergency calls only – Dial 999*
42	† **British Waterways Board** Paddington Toll Office, Delamere Terrace, Paddington, W2 6ND (01-286 6101)	*Moorings, Information, Shop* (M, S, U, W)
42	† **Turner Marinas Ltd** Blomfield Road Moorings, (Office: 57 Fitzroy Road, London, NW1 8TS) (01-722 9806)	*Boatyards and Moorings* (M) *See also under next Section*
42	**'Jason's Trip'** Barge *Tab*, 66 Blomfield Road, London, W9 (01-286 3428)	*Passenger Vessel Operators* (F)
42	**Metropolitan Police** 4 Harrow Road, Paddington Green, W2 (01-725 4212)	*Emergency calls only – Dial 999*

40	**The Grand Junction Arms** *(Inn)*, Acton Lane, Harlesden, NW10 (01-965 5670/6810)
41	**The Narrow Boat** *(Inn)*, 346, Ladbroke Grove, W10 (01-969 5359)
41	**The Carlton Bridge Tavern**, 45 Woodfield Road, London, W9 (01-286 1886)
42	**The Pride of the Canal** *(Inn)*, 64 Alfred Road, London, W2 (01-286 1923)
42	**The Warwick Castle** *(Inn)*, 6 Warwick Place, W9 (01-286 6868/9604)
42	**The Bridge House** *(Hotel)*, 13 Westbourne Terrace Road, W2 (01-286 7925)
42	**The Lace Plate** *(Cruising Restaurant)*, c/o 66 Blomfield Road, London, W9 (01-286 3428)

† British Waterways Board Moorings:

42	'Special' Class – Paddington, Bishops Bridge Road	Category 1
42	– Paddington, Blomfield Road	Category 1
	(Managed by Turner Marinas)	
42	24-hour free moorings – at Delamere Terrace	– – –

Private craft may not moor in Brownings Pool, Little Venice.

Towpath Access Points: Water Road, Alperton; Willings Bridge (No. 10); Steele Road; Acton Lane Bridge (No. 9); Old Oak Lane Bridge (No. 7); Mitre Bridge (No. 6), Scrubs Lane; Kensal Green Bridge (No. 4); Wedlake Street Bridge; Kensal Road/Golborne Road; Carlton Bridge; Harrow Road Bridge (No. 3); Warwick Crescent; Blomfield Road, Paddington Bridge. There is also a gate off Delamere Terrace leading to the BWB Toll Office.

PUBLIC TRANSPORT SERVICES

Railway Services

Station	Region or line	Route	*Normal Frequency
Hayes and Harlington	WR	Paddington–Slough	30 mins
Southall	WR	Paddington–Slough	30 mins
Greenford**	WR	Ealing (Broadway) Branch	60 mins
Greenford	LT	Central Line	12 mins
Alperton	LT	Piccadilly Line	12 mins
Harlesden†	MR	Euston–Watford	20 mins
Willesden Junc.†	MR	Euston–Watford	20 mins
		North London Line – Richmond	20 mins
Kensal Green†	MR	Euston–Watford	20 mins
Westbourne Park**	WR	Paddington–Slough	Peak only
Westbourne Park	LT	Metropolitan (Hammersmith)	8 mins
Royal Oak	LT	Metropolitan (Hammersmith)	8 mins
Warwick Avenue	LT	Bakerloo Line	6 mins
Paddington	WR	Terminus for West Country, South Wales and W. Midlands	–
Paddington	LT	Circle/District	8 mins
		Bakerloo	6 mins
		Metropolitan (Hammersmith)	8 mins

*Not necessarily on Sundays or at 'off-peak' times. **Closed on Sundays.
† Also served at peak times by Bakerloo Line (LT) between Queen's Park and Harrow & Wealdstone.

London Bus Services

Bus route numbers are shown along principal main roads shown on the charts. Bus route terminals are shown with the route number boxed.

Route No.	Termini	Route No.	Termini
6	Kensal Rise Station and Hackney Wick	92	Southall and Wembley Arena
7	Richmond and Tottenham Court Road Station	105	Shepherds Bush and Heathrow Airport
8	Bow Church and Willesden	112	Ealing Broadway and Palmers Green
12	Norwood Junction and Harlesden	120	Hounslow Heath and Greenford Station
15	East Ham and Ladbroke Grove	159	West Hampstead and Thornton Heath
15A	East Ham and Ladbroke Grove	187	South Harrow Station and Queens Park Station
16	Victoria Station and Neasden or Brent Park	195	Charville Lane Estate and Ealing Hospital
16A	Oxford Circus and Brent Cross	205	Park Royal and St Raphael's Estate
18	Sudbury and Kings Cross	207	Uxbridge and Shepherds Bush
27	Archway Station and Richmond	220	Harlesden and Tooting Station
28	Golders Green Station and Wandsworth	226	Golders Green Station and Burnt Oak Broadway
31	Camden Town and Chelsea	232	Hounslow and Yeading
36	Hither Green Station and Queens Park Station	260	North Finchley and Harlesden
36B	Grove Park and Queens Park Station	266	Hammersmith to Cricklewood and Brent Cross
46	Farringdon Street, Kings Cross, Warwick Avenue and Kensal Rise	274	Ealing Broadway Station to Hayes Station and Yeading
52	Victoria Station and Mill Hill Broadway	282	Southall Garage and Mount Vernon Hospital (Northwood)
52A	Victoria Station and Westbourne Park Station		
83	Golders Green Station and Southall		

295	Ladbroke Grove and Clapham Junction
297	Willesden Garage and Ealing Broadway
E2	Ruislip Lido and Brentford

All-Night Bus Services

N18	Liverpool Street or Waterloo, Trafalgar Square and Edgware Station	N56	Paddington Station and Heathrow
N50	Kings Cross, Ladbroke Grove and Greenford	N79	Willesden Garage and Lewisham
N51	Greenford, Ladbroke Grove and Kings Cross	N89	London Bridge and Uxbridge or Southall
		N94	Liverpool Street and Edgware Station

Maps and Publications Free pocket maps
of all London Transport's services as well
as a special tourist information map are
available. Free maps, leaflets and London
Transport books can be obtained from any
London Transport Enquiry Office. These
are at Piccadilly Circus, Oxford Circus,
King's Cross, Euston, Victoria and
St. James's Park Underground stations.
Maps and free leaflets are also available by
post from the Public Relations Officer,
London Transport, 55 Broadway, SW1H OBD.

Rebuilt Lydiard (Aldington Tunnel)

Section 7 Regent's Canal
Paddington to Limehouse

Distance 8 statute land miles and 5 furlongs
Number of Locks 13 (including Limehouse Ship Lock)
Tunnels Maida Hill (272 yards)
Islington (960 yards)
Bridges 58 (including the Regent's Canal Swing Bridge over Lock No. 13 — Limehouse)
Branches Cumberland Basin; St Pancras Basin; Battlebridge (or Horsfall) Basin; City Road Basin; Wenlock Basin; Kingsland Basin; Hertford Union (Duckett's) Canal and Limehouse Basin (Regent's Canal Dock) — leading to the Limehouse Cut.

Status As Section 5 (except Limehouse Basin — See note under Section 8)
Maximum dimensions of craft:
Headroom 8'11" (Originally constructed to pass craft at 9'9")
Length 78'0" (Originally constructed to pass craft of 80'0")
Beam 14'3" (Originally constructed to pass craft of 14'6")
Draught 3'6" (Originally constructed to pass craft at 4'6")

Ship Lock (Limehouse No. 13) only
This lock gives access to the Limehouse Basin, from the River Thames.
Length: 350'0"
Width: 60'0"
Depth of sill on HWS: 24'0" (inner): 29'0" approx. (outer)
Maximum dimensions of craft accepted in basin: 300'0" × 45'0" × 16'0"

Waterway Authority (for navigation) For details see preamble to Section 5.
Regent's Section Engineer
British Waterways Board,
Pierhead Office, Limehouse Basin, Narrow Street, London, E14 8DN
(Tel: 01-790 3444)

Licensing See preamble to Section 5.

SPEED LIMIT THROUGHOUT — 4 mph.

PUBLIC ACCESS TO TOWING PATH
In collaboration with the London Boroughs affected, the British Waterways Board has opened the towing path along the Regent's Canal, from Lisson Grove Bridge to Islington Tunnel (Western End) and from Islington Tunnel (Eastern End) to Commercial Road Lock (No. 12). These sections are designated 'Canalside' Walks' and are opened to the public from 8.00 am daily except Sundays

123

and Bank Holidays when they are opened at 10.00 am until half an hour before dusk. Overnight the access gates are padlocked.

You should note, therefore that the opening of these towpaths does not confer any public right of way. Cycling along the towpath is only possible on receipt of the necessary permit. Full details are obtainable from the London Area Engineer's Office of the Board at: 43, Clarendon Road, Watford, Herts WD1 1JE (0923) 31363. Details of fishing from the towpath can be obtained from the Licensing Supervisor at the address shown on page 91. Swimming in the canals is prohibited.

Those in charge of craft using the navigation can obtain access to and from the street across the towing path out of hours at certain designated points by means of the standard pattern BWB sanitary station key. These are at Little Venice (Delamere Terrace); Camden Lock; St Pancras Lock (off Camley Street); City Road Lock (off Graham Street); Old Ford Lock (Old Ford Road); and Salmon Lane Lock (No. 11), Tomlins Terrace. There is also access at Parnell Road Bridge above the top lock on the Hertford Union Canal.

Warning to small craft concerning rubbish
Considerable quantities of rubbish may be encountered in the Regent's Canal. Please read the notes on page 155.

Regent's Canal and the Earl of Snowdon's Aviary at London Zoo

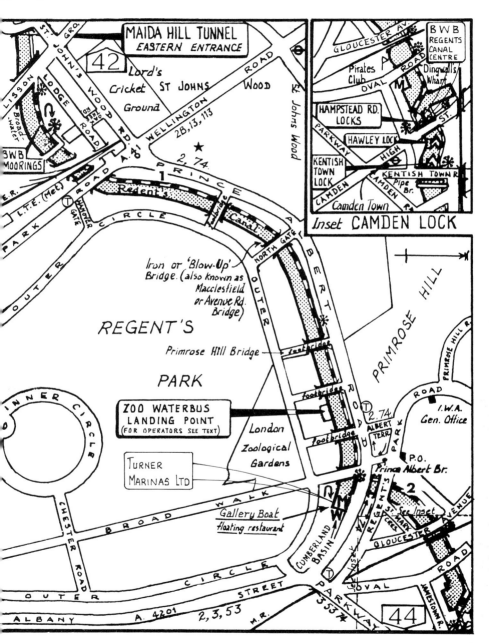

Cumberland Basin - Regent's Canal

Regent's Canal - Towpath Bridge at Dingwall's Wharf Camden Town

Regent's Canal - Hampstead Road Locks

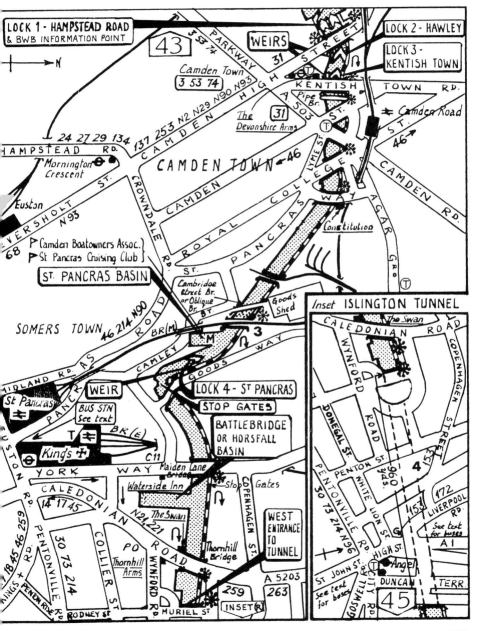

Lock rise (or fall)	Lock Name and No.		Falls from	Rises from
8′0″ (Paired)	Hampstead Road (also known as Camden Lock)	(1)	Little Venice	Limehouse Basin
8′0″	Hawley	(2)	Little Venice	Limehouse Basin
8′0″	Kentish Town	(3)	Little Venice	Limehouse Basin
8′0″	St Pancras	(4)	Little Venice	Limehouse Basin

The stop gates at Goods Way and Maiden Lane Bridge for flood prevention of the King's Cross railway tunnels have now been removed. All locks worked by boat crews.

CHART DIRECTORY (Charts 43 and 44)

For key to letter references see p. 21

British Waterways Board
Headquarters, Melbury House, Melbury Terrace, London, NW1 6JX
(Adjacent to Marylebone Station)
(01-262 6711)

Information, Book and Guide sales etc.
Lock paddle windlasses for sale

Turner Marinas Ltd
43 Lisson Grove Moorings,
43 Cumberland Basin,
(Office at: 57 Fitzroy Road, London, NW1 8TS) (01-722 9806)

Boatyards and Moorings
(C, M, W, U)
(C, E, G, M, U, W)

43 **Metropolitan Police**
20½ Newcourt Street, London, NW8
(01-725 4212)

Emergency calls only – dial 999

43 **Inland Waterways Association Ltd**
114 Regent's Park Road,
London, NW1 8UQ
(01-586 2556/2510)

Book and chart sales
Information

43 **The Pirate Club**
Pirates Castle, Oval Road,
Camden Town, NW1
(01-267 6605)

Youth Club

43/44 **Jenny Wren Cruises**
Dingwalls Wharf, 250 Camden High Street,
NW1 (01-485 4433)

Passenger Vessel Operators
(F)
Also 'My Fair Lady' Floating Restaurant

43/44 **London Waterbus Co.**
Dingwalls Wharf, Camden High Street,
London, NW1 8AF (01-482 2550)

Passenger Vessel Operators
(Zoo Waterbus)
(F)

43/44	**British Waterways Board** Hampstead Road Locks, Camden High Street, NW1 (01-485 2923)*	*Lock-keeper's Office* (W) *Lock worked by boat crews*
43/44	**British Waterways Board** Hampstead Road Locks, Camden High Street, London, NW1 (01-482 0523)	*Information Centre*
44	**Metropolitan Police** 12A Holmes Road, Kentish Town, NW5 (01-725 4212)	*Emergency calls only – Dial 999*
44	†**St Pancras Cruising Club** St Pancras Yacht Basin, Camley Street, London, NW1 (01-278 2805)	*Yacht Basin and Club* (ATYC) (M, S, U, W)
44	**British Waterways Board** St Pancras Lock, Camley Street, London, NW1	Lock worked by boat crews

43 **The Gallery Boat** *(Floating Restaurant)*, Cumberland Basin, NW1 (01-485 8137)
44 **Le Routier** *(Lockside Restaurant)*, Commercial Place, London, NW1 (Camden Lock) (01-485 0360)
43 **My Fair Lady** *(Restaurant motor barge)*, 250 Camden High St, NW1 (01-485 4433)
43/44 **The Devonshire Arms** *(Inn)*, 33 Kentish Town Road, NW1 (01-485 2079)
44 **The Constitution** *(Inn)*, 42 St Pancras Way, London, NW1 (01-387 4805)
44 **The Swan** *(Inn)*, Thornhill Bridge, 125 Caledonian Road, NW1 (01-837 1924)
44 **The Waterside Inn**, 82 York Way, N1 (01-837 7118)
44 **The Thornhill Arms**, Caledonian Road, N1
(A) **C. Birch & Son**, 207 Royal College Street, NW1 (01-485 9087) *Fishing tackle*

†**British Waterways Board Moorings:**
'Special' Class sites – St Pancras Yacht Basin   Category 1

*If no reply from this number, all enquiries should be directed to the Regent's Section Inspector's Office at Limehouse (01-790 3444). *See page 139.*

Public Towpath Lisson Grove to Islington Tunnel
Access Points: Lisson Grove Bridge; Paveley Street Estate footbridge; Prince Albert Road, Chalbert Street footbridge; Prince Albert Road, Primrose Hill Bridge; Prince Albert Bridge, Cumberland Basin; Gloucester Avenue; Oval Road (Pirates Castle); Dingwall's Wharf, Camden High Street Bridge; Kentish Town Road Bridge, Devonshire Arms; Royal College Street; St Pancras Way, Constitution (Inn); Maiden Lane Bridge, York Way; Thornhill Bridge, Caledonian Road, The Swan Inn; Muriel Street, Islington.

Note: There is no towpath through Maida Hill or Islington Tunnels, Canoes and unpowered craft are prohibited navigation through Islington Tunnel.

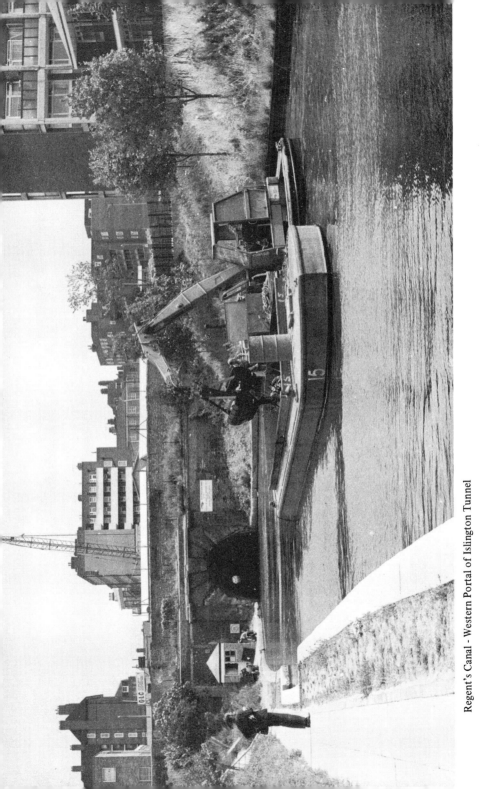

Regent's Canal - Western Portal of Islington Tunnel

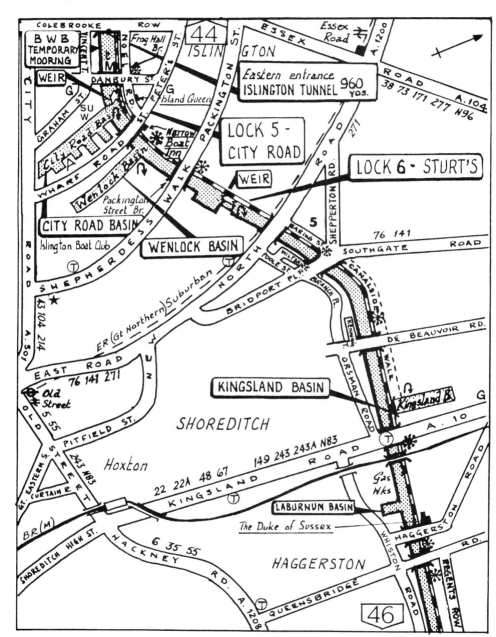

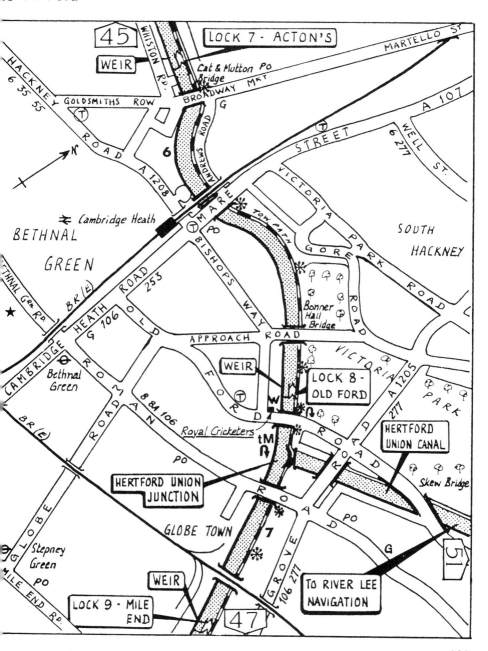

Hertford Union Canal runs by Victoria Park   *Photo: Derek Pratt*

Lock rise (or fall)	Lock Name and No.		Falls from	Rises from
8'0''	City Road	(5)	Little Venice	Limehouse Basin
8'0''	Sturt's	(6)	Little Venice	Limehouse Basin
8'0''	Acton's	(7)	Little Venice	Limehouse Basin
8'0''	Old Ford (Regent's)	(8)	Little Venice	Limehouse Basin

All locks worked by boat crews. For details of Mile End Lock see page 134.

CHART DIRECTORY (Charts 45 and 46)
For key to letter references see p. 21

| 45 | **British Waterways Board** City Road Lock, Graham Street, Islington, N1 | *Lock-keeper's office* (M, S, W) Lock worked by boat crews |

45 **Islington Boat Club** *Youth Club*
City Road, London, N1 (01-253 0778)

45 **Metropolitan Police** *Emergency calls only – Dial 999*
4 Shepherdess Walk, London, N1
(01-488 5212)

46 **Metropolitan Police** *Emergency calls only – Dial 999*
458 Bethnal Green Road, London, E2
(01-488 5212)

46 **British Waterways Board** *Lock-keeper's office*
Old Ford Lock, Old Ford Road, (M, W)
Victoria Park, London, E3
(01-980 1426)* Lock worked by boat crews

(A) **J. Mitchell**, 410 Kingsland Road, E8 (01-254 9333) *Fishing tackle*
The Narrow Boat *(Inn)*, 119 St Peter's Street, London, N1 (01-226 3906)
The Island Queen *(Inn)*, 87 Noel Road, Islington, London, N1 (01-226 5507)
The Royal Cricketers *(Inn)*, 211 Old Ford Road, E2 (01-980 3259)
The Duke of Sussex *(Inn)*, 151 Haggerston Road, E8 (01-254 4271)
Public Towpath Islington Tunnel to Commercial Road
Access Points: Frog Hall Bridge (Danbury Street); Narrow Boat Inn;
Packington Street Bridge; Baring Street; Whitmore Bridge
(De Beauvoir Road); Kingsland Road; Haggerston Road (The
Duke of Sussex); Queensbridge Road, Regents Row; Cat and
Mutton Bridge; Mare Street; Victoria Park (above Bonner Hall
Bridge); Old Ford Lock (2); Old Ford Road (opposite The
Royal Cricketers); Roman Road Bridge; Mile End Park
(Cordova Road).

*If no reply from this number, all enquiries should be directed to the Regent's Section
Inspector's Office at Limehouse (01-790 3444). *See page 139.*

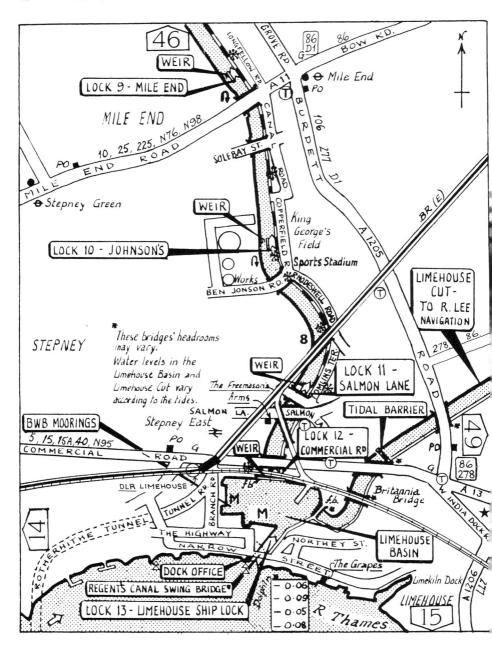

Lock rise (or fall)	Lock Name and No.		Falls from	Rises from
8'0''	Mile End	(9)	Little Venice	Limehouse Basin
8'0''	Johnson's	(10)	Little Venice	Limehouse Basin
8'0''	Salmon Lane	(11)	Little Venice	Limehouse Basin
Variable according to level in Basin.	Commercial Road	(12)	Little Venice	Limehouse Basin
Between 9'0'' and 12'0'' according to tide, to level. (HWS)	Limehouse Ship Lock	(13)	Limehouse Basin	River Thames

Locks 9–12 worked by boat crews.

CHART DIRECTORY

For key to letter references see p. 21

British Waterways Board
Mile End Lock, Longfellow Road, London, E3

Lock worked by boat crews.

British Waterways Board
Salmon Lane Lock, Tomlin's Terrace, Salmon Lane, London, E14 (01-987 1963)*

Lock-keeper's office.
Lock worked by boat crews.

British Waterways Board
Commercial Road Lock, Commercial Road, London, E14

Lock worked by boat crews.

British Waterways Board
Pierhead Office, Limehouse Basin, Narrow Street, London, E14 8DN (01-790 3444)
Out of hours (01-478 4824)

Dock Manager's Office, Lock-keeper (Ship Lock), Bridge-keeper, Regent's Section Inspector. (M)†
Lock worked only by keeper.

Metropolitan Police
111 Bow Road, London, E3 (01-488 5212)

Emergency calls only – Dial 999.

Metropolitan Police
29 West India Dock Road, London, E14 (01-488 5212)

Emergency calls only – Dial 999.

Metropolitan Police
Thames Division, 98 Wapping High Street, E1 9NE (01-488 5291)

Police Patrols in River Thames.

The Freemason's Arms *(Inn),* 98 Salmon Lane, London, E14 (01-987 1102)
The Grapes *(Inn),* 76 Narrow Street, London, E14 (01-987 4396)

† British Waterways Board Moorings :
'Special' Class – Limehouse Basin
*If no reply from this number, contact 01-790 3444.

Regent's Canal - Mile End Lock

Limehouse Ship Lock entrance from the River Thames

ENTRY TO THE LONDON CANALS SYSTEM AT LIMEHOUSE

All passages must be notified in advance to the Dockmaster's office.
Entry to the canal system described in this guide from the River Thames is
possible at three points. Access via Brentford Creek into the Grand Union Canal
(Main Line), formerly the Grand Junction Canal, has already been described on
pages 92 – 93.

The second point of access is described here in conjunction with Chart No. 47.
(see also the Key to the East London charts at the start of Section 8).

Originally there were three access locks from the River Thames at this point.
Upstream of the present Ship Lock into Limehouse Basin (formerly known as
Regent's Canal Dock) there was a Barge Lock, 79'0" long by 14'6" wide. This
has now been filled in. All craft wishing to pass between the Limehouse Basin
and the River Thames in either direction, must therefore use the Ship Lock
which is 350'0" long by 60'0" wide. Downstream of the Ship Lock on the other
side of Northey Street was the old Limehouse Barge Lock which only gave access
to the Limehouse Cut, which had been constructed by the Lee Conservancy to
short-cut the tortuous passage via Bow Creek and Blackwall and Limehouse
Reaches for lighter traffic bound for the Pool of London. There was no inter-
connection by water between the Cut and the Basin for some years as there is
today although there was when the basin was first built. This latter lock was
88'0" long by 19'0" wide. The river entrance is still visible but the cut has been
filled in between Northey Street and Narrow Street.

Limehouse Ship Lock (No. 13)

This lock is mechanically operated in conjunction with the Regent's Canal Swing
Bridge, which crosses it carrying Narrow Street. Being a tidal lock it can only be
worked at certain states of the tide in the River Thames, and to conserve the
level maintained in the Limehouse Basin it is therefore operated on request in
advance (Tel: 01-790 3444) from about 3 hours before High Water up to High
Water at the Lock Entrance, which occurs about 5 or 6 minutes before High
Water at London Bridge. *After High Tide the Ship Lock is closed.*

Craft arriving after High Water or prior to the above opening times will not
find it convenient to moor locally to the pierhead, which is on the upstream
side, but should arrange to moor at some convenient place, such as Tower Pier,
or by arrangement with the lessees, at Cherry Garden Pier, Tunnel (Wapping) Pier,
West India Dock Pier, or off St Katharine Yacht Haven. *See pages 67 – 73 for
details and telephone numbers.*

Craft not intending to navigate the canal system, being of larger dimensions
than the system will accommodate, may be accepted through the Ship Lock for
the purpose of temporary mooring in the basin if they so wish. The normal
dimensions of craft accepted for this purpose are 300'0" o'all length × 45'0"
beam, drawing a maximum of 16'0". Full details of mooring arrangements and
fees are obtainable on application to the Dockmaster, Pierhead Office, Lime-

house Basin, Narrow Street, London, E14 8DN (01-790 3444).

A blue flag is normally flown at the masthead of the flagstaff on the Limehouse Lock pierhead when the lock is workable. If a red flag is flown stand clear as this signifies craft are leaving the lock. A dolphin is located downstream of the lock entrance to which vessels may berth temporarily for this purpose.

Entry to Regent's Canal and Lee Navigation (via Hertford Union Canal)
Having negotiated the Ship Lock, craft bound for the Regent's Canal should proceed ahead in a northerly direction and enter Commercial Road Lock (No. 12), leaving the coal jetty to starboard (on their right). Craft bound for the Lee Navigation by this route, proceed by Locks 12, 11, 10 and 9 (Commercial Road to Mile End) to a point 3½ furlongs above Mile End Lock where they turn right into the Hertford Union Canal, just below Old Ford Locks.

Entry to Lee Navigation (via Limehouse Cut)
On entering the Limehouse Basin, keep right and leave the coal jetty on your left to enter the Cut on the eastern side of the basin. However, you should be warned that the Cut is partially tidal due to the action of tides in the River Lee backwaters and operation of Bow Tidal Locks which are at the head of the Cut. Before proceeding by this route it is advisable to contact the **BWB Office at Bow** Locks (01-987 5661) to ascertain the traffic and water conditions. You may note from Section 8 of this guide that the Lee Navigation (including the Limehouse Cut) is still classified as a Commercial Waterway so that you may meet tugs or tractors with trains of lighters in this section.

You should also be warned that above Bow Locks such bridges as Three Mills Bridge and the Northern Outfall Sewer Aqueduct have a restricted headroom on high tides, and if you are in any doubt about your craft's ability to clear these bridges you should use the alternative route via the Hertford Union Canal, which joins the Lee Navigation above Old Ford Locks on the River Lee. (Chart No. 50).

Note that you should not confuse the Old Ford (Regent's) Lock, which is above the western junction of the Hertford Union Canal, with the similarly named Old Ford (Lee) Locks, below the eastern junction.

Full details of the Limehouse Cut and its junction with the Lee Navigation at Bromley-by-Bow are shown in Chart No. 49. Old Ford (Lee) Locks and the eastern Hertford Union Junction are shown in Chart No. 51.

Exit from the Ship Lock
Exit times are the same as for entry. To await the lock opening, you may temporarily moor in the Limehouse Basin, by permission of the Dockmaster, or a more comfortable mooring may be found below Old Ford (Regent's) Lock just above the Hertford Union Canal Junction.

If leaving by the Limehouse Cut route, a temporary mooring may be found in the Hackney Cut above Old Ford Locks.

Tidal Barrier (Limehouse Cut)

In connection with the Thames Tidal Barrier and the Thames Flood Prevention Scheme, there is a tidal barrier consisting of an overhead sluice gate which lowers into the Cut, just above Britannia Bridge. The barrier will only be lowered to prevent passage at exceptional high tides. Warnings that the barrier is in operation will be given to all craft by the lock-keepers at Old Ford (Lee) Locks and at the Limehouse Ship Lock, who will prohibit craft from proceeding until the barrier has been re-opened.

Regent's Canal Swing Bridge

This swing bridge, which carries Narrow Street across the Limehouse Ship Lock will be swung to admit or release shipping in conjunction with the operation of the lock. On certain high tides, the Ship Lock may be opened completely giving direct access from the river into the basin. Do not proceed at full speed in such cases through the lock. Allow the bridgeman time to open the bridge. If entering the Basin you will also have to check that your craft is licensed with the Dockmaster, before clearing the top gates.

Licensing

If you have not previously licensed your craft to navigate on British Waterways Board waterways, you may complete the necessary formalities at the Dockmaster's office, during normal business hours (0800 — 1700) Monday to Friday.

PUBLIC TRANSPORT SERVICES

Railway Services

Station	Region or line	Route	*Normal Frequency
Warwick Avenue	LT	Bakerloo Line	6 mins
Paddington	WR	Terminus for West Country, South Wales and W. Midlands	—
Paddington	LT	Circle/District	6 mins
		Bakerloo	6 mins
		Metropolitan (Hammersmith)	8 mins
Marylebone	MR	Terminus for High Wycombe & Aylesbury Lines	—
	LT	Bakerloo Line	6 mins
St John's Wood	LT	Fleet	6 mins
Baker Street	LT	Metropolitan Lines (All)	6 mins
		Circle	6 mins
		Bakerloo	6 mins
		Fleet	6 mins
Camden Town	LT	Northern Lines (All)	3/4 mins
Mornington Crescent	LT	Northern Line (West End Branch)	6/8 mins
Camden Road	MR	North Woolwich — Richmond	20 mins

Station	Region or line	Route	*Normal Frequency
Euston	MR	Terminus for Midlands, North-West and Scotland	–
	LT	Northern Lines (West End & City)	6 mins
		Victoria	4 mins
St Pancras	MR	Terminus for Midlands	–
King's Cross	ER	Terminus for Midlands, North-East and Scotland	–
	MR	Midland/City Line	30 mins
	LT	Piccadilly Line	6 mins
		Victoria Line	4 mins
		Northern Line (City Branch)	6 mins
		Circle/Metropolitan	6 mins
Caledonian Road & Barnsbury	MR	North Woolwich – Richmond	20 mins
Angel (Islington)	LT	Northern Line (City Branch)	6 mins
Essex Road	ER	Great Northern Electrics	30 mins
Old Street	LT	Northern Line (City Branch)	6 mins
Old Street	ER	Great Northern Electrics	30 mins
Cambridge Heath	ER	Liverpool Street – Enfield	20 mins
Bethnal Green	LT	Central Line	10 mins
Stepney Green	LT	District/Metropolitan†	12/15 mins
Mile End	LT	District/Metropolitan†	12/15 mins
		Central Line	10 mins
Bow Road	LT	District Metropolitan†	12/15 mins
Stepney East	ER	Fenchurch Street – Upminster	20 mins

*Not necessarily on Sundays or at 'off-peak' times.
†Metropolitan Line trains only run at peak times. Change at Whitechapel.

Docklands Light Railway (opening Summer 1987)

Stations: Limehouse, Westferry
(FOR OTHER STATIONS SEE SECTIONS 4 AND 8) Enquiries: LDDC (01-515 3000)

London Bus Services

As far as has been practicable, bus route numbers have been shown along principal main roads on the charts. Bus route terminals are shown with the route number boxed. Due to the concentration of routes in the Central London area, however, the route numbers omitted from the charts are shown below in relation to buses terminating at King's Cross Bus Station and those routes passing Angel Underground Station which cross the Islington Tunnel.

Routes terminating at King's Cross – **45, 63, 77A, 221, C11, N50, N51, N56.**

Angel (Islington)
4, 19, 30, 38, 43, 73, 153, 171, 263A, 277, 279, 279A, N92, N96.

Route No.	Termini	Route No.	Termini
2	West Norwood, Baker Street Station and London Zoo	5	Becontree Heath and Old Street
		6	Kensal Rise Station and Hackney Wick
2B	Crystal Palace and Golders Green	8	Bow Church and Willesden
3	Crystal Palace and Camden Town	8A	Old Ford and London Bridge Station
4	Tufnell Park and Waterloo	10	Victoria Station and Wanstead

13	Aldwych and North Finchley
14	Hornsey Rise and Putney
15	East Ham and Ladbroke Grove
16	Victoria Station and Neasden
16A	Oxford Circus and Brent Cross
17	North Finchley and London Bridge Station
18	Sudbury and Kings Cross
19	Tooting Bec Station and Finsbury Park
22	Putney Common and Homerton
22A	Clapton Park and Wapping Station
23	East Ham and Ladbroke Grove
24	Hampstead Heath and Pimlico
25	Ilford and Victoria Station
26	Barnet, Golders Green and Brent Cross
27	Archway Station and Richmond
29	Victoria Station and Enfield
30	Putney Heath and Hackney Wick
31	Camden Town and Chelsea
35	Clapham Common and Clapton Park
38	Victoria Station and Leyton Green
40	Herne Hill and Poplar
43	London Bridge Station and Friern Barnet
45	South Kensington, Kings Cross and Archway Station
46	Farringdon Street and Kensal Rise
48	London Bridge and Leyton Green
53	Parliament Hill Fields and Plumstead Common
55	Victoria Station and Whipps Cross
67	Wood Green and Aldgate
68	Chalk Farm and South Croydon
73	Stoke Newington and Hammersmith
74	Camden Town and Putney Heath
76	Victoria Station and Northumberland Park
77A	Kings Cross and Wandsworth
106	Finsbury Park and Isle of Dogs
113	Edgware Station and Oxford Circus
134	Barnet Church and Tottenham Court Road Station
137	Crystal Palace, Oxford Circus and Archway
141	Wood Green, Farringdon Street and Grove Park
149	Edmonton, Liverpool Street and Waterloo
153	Archway and Tottenham Court Road
159	West Hampstead and Thornton Heath
171	Forest Hill and Rosebery Avenue

176	Willesden and Forest Hill
214	Parliament Hill Fields and Moorgate
221	Holborn Circus and Edgware Station
243	Wood Green and Holborn Circus
243A	Wood Green and Liverpool Street Station
253	Aldgate, Finsbury Park and Warren Street Station
259	Hammond Street and Holborn Circus
263A	North Finchley and Liverpool Street Station
271	Highgate Village and Moorgate
277	Poplar, Angel and Smithfield
279	Waltham Cross and Smithfield
279A	Waltham Cross and Liverpool Street Station
C11	Brent Cross, West Hampstead and Kings Cross
D1	Docklands Clipper: Mile End — Limehouse and Poplar

All-Night Bus Routes

N2	Friern Barnet and Crystal Palace
N11	Hackney Wick, Trafalgar Square and Acton
N13	Trafalgar Square and Barnet
N18	Liverpool Street Station and Edgware
N21	Trafalgar Square and North Finchley
N29	Trafalgar Square and Enfield
N50	Kings Cross, Ladbroke Grove and Greenford (Westbound)
N51	Greenford, Ladbroke Grove and Kings Cross (Eastbound)
N56	Paddington, Kings Cross and Heathrow (Circular)
N76	Trafalgar Square and Wanstead
N79	Willesden, Trafalgar Square and Lewisham
N83	Trafalgar Square and Wanstead
N90	Victoria and Hammond Street
N92	Trafalgar Square and Muswell Hill
N93	Fulwell, Trafalgar Square and Hampstead Heath
N94	Liverpool Street and Edgware
N95	Victoria Station and Dagenham
N96	Waterloo Station and Chingford
N98	Victoria Station and Harold Hill

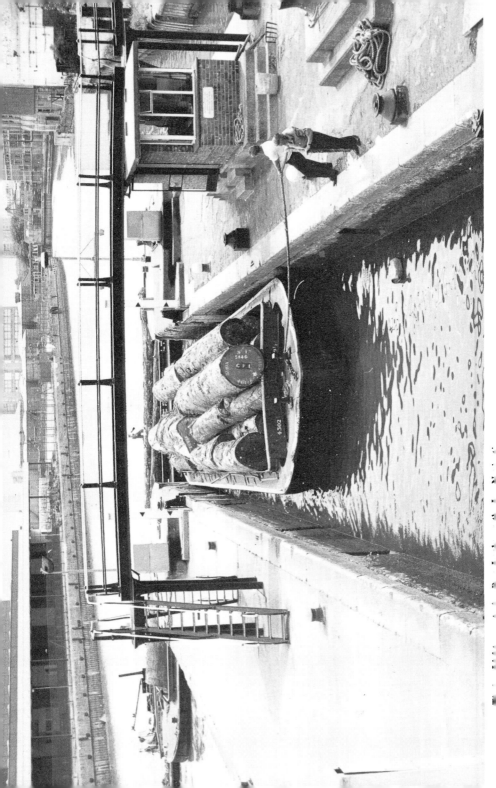

Part III
The Lee Navigation

**British
Waterways
Board**

River Lee - The Clock Mill at Three Mills   *Photo: Derek Pratt*

Section 8 **Lee Navigation**
Bow Creek to Waltham Lock

GENERAL

The River Lee is probably as old as the River Thames as a navigable waterway, and, like the Thames, was still a commercial route until recently for lighter and barge traffic, particularly in the lower reaches, which this guide covers. The chief cargoes were timber and copper.

The busiest section was that which ran from Limehouse Lock, now closed and filled in, up to Ponders End and Brimsdown, but, as explained in Section 7, the channel into the Limehouse Basin was restored, so that the route now shares a common exit into the Thames by way of the Limehouse Ship Lock – the only lock remaining of the three originally constructed.

There are two other routes also into the Lee Navigation, those provided by the River Lee's own estuary – Bow Creek – which is linked to the northern end of the Limehouse Cut at Bow Tidal Locks, and by the connecting waterway with the Regent's Canal at Old Ford – the Hertford Union Canal – which was constructed in 1830 at the instigation of Sir George Duckett, and hence came to be known as 'Duckett's Canal'.

Being a river, although canalised in many sections, this waterway is more liable to the vagaries of the weather, and special mention should be made of the liability to flooding throughout the length of the navigation we are describing. Flooding in the upper sections above Tottenham will affect the bridge headrooms, and perhaps more importantly the amount of control that a skipper of a small craft will have over his course downstream, which may be important if meeting oncoming traffic.

If the river goes into flood it is probably wise to tie up out of harm's way and await quieter conditions before proceeding again. Official mooring places are few and far between on the lower river but in doubt, one should seek the assistance of the lock-keepers in this respect. By using this guide one will be in touch with one's surroundings and if it is necessary to leave your cruiser for a period the public transport information should be of assistance in providing an alternative means of transport home.

Below Enfield the river is rather drab and industrialised, but above this point the scenery becomes more rural and the upper reaches will be a delight to the cruising man in search of peace and solitude in such areas as Dobb's Weir on the main river, or Roydon and Little Hallingbury on the River Stort, which joins the Lee at Feilde's Lock.

The limits of navigation are: River Lee – Hertford,
River Stort – Bishop's Stortford.

SPEED LIMIT THROUGHOUT – 4 m.p.h.

Distance	Bow Creek to Waltham Town Lock — 14 miles 5 furlongs
Number of Locks	10 (including Bow Tidal Locks)
Tunnels	None
Bridges	46 (not incl. access bridges at paired locks)
Branches	Limehouse Cut (1 mile 6 furlongs); *Three Mills Wall River;
	*Bow Back River; *Old River Lee; *City Mill River;
	*Waterworks River; *Channelsea River; Hertford Union
	Canal (1 mile 1½ furlongs — including 3 locks).
Status	Commercial (Transport Act, 1968)

Maximum Dimensions of craft

Bow Creek or Limehouse Basin to Old Ford		*Hertford Union Canal*	
Headroom	8'0" (at minimum water level)	*Headroom*	8'0"
Length	90'0"	*Length*	84'0"
Beam	19'6"	*Beam*	14'5"
Draught	5'0" (at minimum water level)	*Draught*	3'6"

Old Ford to Enfield

Headroom	7'3" (at average summer level at Lea Bridge)
Length	85'0"
Beam	18'0"
Draught	5'0"

Enfield to Waltham Lock (and also to Hertford)

Headroom	7'3" (at average summer level)
Length	85'0"
Beam	13'3"
Draught	4'9"

Waterway Authority (for navigation) For details see preamble to Section 5.
Lee Section Inspector
British Waterways Board,
Enfield Yard, Ordnance Road, Enfield Lock, Middx (Lea Valley 764626).

Other Authorities concerned with the river

Lea Valley Regional Park Authority
Myddelton House, Bulls Cross, Enfield, Middx
(Lea Valley 717711)

Promoting water sports at centres along the navigation.

Thames Water Authority (Lea Division)
The Grange, Crossbrook Street, Waltham Cross,
Essex (Waltham Cross 23611)

River Management, Tidal Barriers, etc. Angling.

Licensing See preamble to Section 5
Licences may also be issued during business hours from Monday to Friday at
the Dockmaster's office, Pierhead Office, Limehouse Basin, Narrow Street,
London, E14 8DN (01-790 3444), or at the lock-keeper's office, Bow Locks,
Bromley-by-Bow, London, E3 (01-987 5661).

*These branches are partially navigable according to the tides.

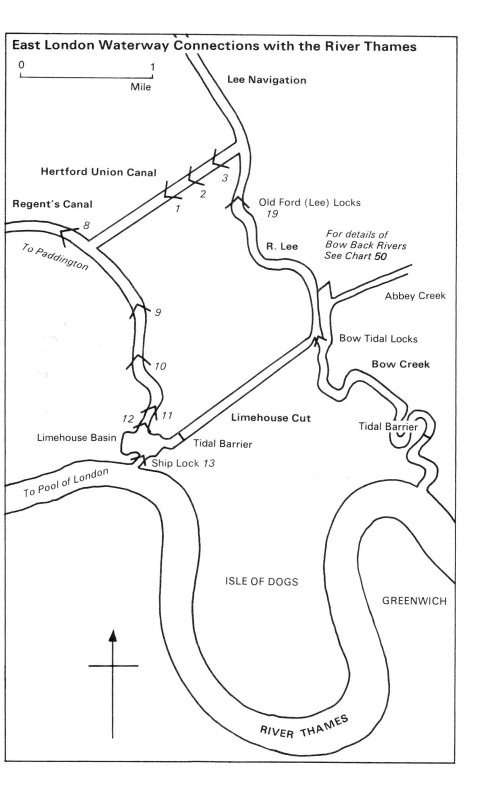

ENTRY TO THE RIVER LEE NAVIGATION FROM THE RIVER THAMES

The safest route for small craft wishing to visit the River Lee from the Upper Thames is to proceed from Teddington to Brentford, enter the Grand Union Canal and ascend the main line as far as Bull's Bridge Junction. Follow the Paddington Arm to Little Venice and enter the Regent's Canal, descending to the Hertford Union Junction, just below Old Ford Lock (Regent's) (No. 8). Entry to the Lee Navigation is then effected by using the Hertford Union Canal and joining the Lee Navigation above Old Ford Locks (No. 19), thus avoiding any waiting time for tidal working at Limehouse or Bow. Details of the two junctions in the Regent's Canal and the Lee Navigation are shown on Charts **46** and **51** respectively. The Regent's Canal Junction is not very obvious, looking like one of the many small dock entries that abound in this part of the canal.

By this means, one may join and leave the River Lee at times when commercial traffic is light, since such traffic is dictated by the tides in the River Thames and Bow Creek. You should therefore time entry and exit of the Hertford Union at around Low Water at London Bridge.

Sturdier craft may wish to cruise the Lower Thames down to Limehouse. After locking through the Limehouse Ship Lock (No. 13) as described on page 143 in the previous section, one may again avoid the traffic in the Limehouse Cut and the tidal Lee Navigation, by using the Regent's Canal up to the Hertford Union Junction and joining the Lee by the above-mentioned route. If you decide to use the Limehouse Cut, you should consult the notes on page 144 in the previous section.

Prior arrangement with the lock-keeper at Bow Locks is essential by telephoning 01-987 5661. You should note that these locks are only worked from 4 hours *before* to 2 hours *after* High Water (London Bridge) on all tides, but night passage is unwise. Passage up to Bow Locks through the Creek at Low Water is not possible. Mooring in the Thames prior to entry or after leaving Bow Creek may be effected off Greenwich Yacht Club which lies on the South (Surrey) bank in the bight between Bugsby's and Woolwich Reaches. Anchoring is possible in Bugsby's Reach just off Redpath Dorman Long Ltd's premises in River Way, or it may be possible to tie up alongside a barge road for the night but this must be arranged with the owners or their roadsman direct. Further information may be obtained from the Thames Barrier Navigation Centre or the Assistant Harbour Master. See pages 78 and 67 respectively for contact details.

Bow Creek Tidal Barrier

In connection with the Thames Tidal Barrier and the Thames Flood Prevention Scheme, there is a tidal barrier consisting of overhead sluices in the lower reach of Bow Creek, adjacent to Victoria Dock Road. The barrier will only be lowered to prevent passage at exceptional high tides. Warnings that the barrier is in operation will be given to all craft by the lock-keepers at Old Ford and Bow, who will prohibit craft from proceeding into Bow Creek until the barrier has been re-opened. The tidal barrier at Britannia Bridge in the Limehouse Cut will also be operated at such times. The barrier is under the control of the Thames Water Authority (Lea Division). Telephone number: Waltham Cross 27881/27889.

Warning to small craft concerning rubbish

A considerable amount of floating rubbish, including plastic sacks, etc. which lurk below the surface, is brought into the lower reaches of the River Lee, the Limehouse Cut and the Limehouse Basin by the tides from the river. Higher up the canal sections, rubbish is also encountered which is illegally jettisoned into the waterways by the unthinking public. This also applies to most of the Regent's Canal below Camden Town.

While dumb lighters ride through such rubbish, and their tugs with their large propellers can chop their way through unscathed, the smaller and shallower sterngear of the pleasure cruiser can be jammed or clogged to the point where the cruiser becomes a powerless hulk and a risk of collision is probable.

Always proceed with caution, keeping a good look-out for such rubbish. The technique of navigating ahead for short periods and being prepared to change gear into neutral or reverse has much to recommend it. If you encounter rubbish, allow the engine to run in neutral while the boat drifts over or through it before re-engaging gear.

If your sterngear is jammed, the cruiser should be moved to the tow-path side, out of the main navigation channel, and bow-hauled if necessary.

THE BOW BACK RIVERS (Chart 50)

The Bow Back Rivers consist of the various part-tidal channels forming the outlets of the River Lee into Bow Creek. Bow Creek is fully tidal from its commencement at Three Mills Sluice to the River Thames. A half furlong below its upper limit it is joined on the left by Abbey Creek which is fully tidal and was navigable on high tides up as far as the site of Abbey Mill Lock, which lies in the mouth of the Channelsea River. The creek and the Channelsea River are no longer navigable above the point where they are crossed by the Northern Outfall Sewer.

The other rivers are approachable only from the Lee Navigation above Bow Locks as follows:

Joining the main navigation immediately above Bow Bridge the Bow Back River, formerly known as St Thomas's Creek, is navigable as far as the head of City Mill Lock, via Marshgate Lock, both of which are no longer used. On the south bank between Pudding Mill Lane and Blaker Road bridges is the City Mills Yacht Club site, details of which may be obtained from the address given in the directory section.

From the tail of Old Ford Locks (No. 19) one may also navigate around High Water up the Old River Lee, leaving the locks on one's left. On the right hand is the entrance to Pudding Mill River, which is theoretically navigable for about half a mile. The next entrance, also on the right, is into the City Mill River which is theoretically navigable downstream into the Bow Back River at the head of City Mill Lock. The small channel to the left just before the lock leads to City Mill Sluice which discharges into the Three Mills Wall River. It is not navigable. Due to tidal flows meeting in this river via the Bow Back River and the Old River Lee, however, there is considerable silting and only very small craft drawing less than 2 ft. can occasionally navigate the full circuit at High Water.

The Old River Lee continues to the head of Carpenters Road Lock which gives access on the right to the Waterworks River which is (again theoretically) navigable as far as West Ham Waterworks (about 4 furlongs). However, Carpenters Road Lock, which consisted of radial gates, is no longer operable.

Three Mills Wall River from the tail of City Mill Sluice to Three Mills Sluice at the head of Bow Creek; Prescott Channel, from Three Mills Wall River to Prescott Sluice at Abbey Creek; the Channelsea River above the Northern Outfall Sewer; and the Old River Lee above Carpenter's Road Lock are now unnavigable, although it may be possible to clear the sluices in very shallow draught craft on high spring tides, but this is not advisable and certainly not by unaccompanied canoeists, etc.

Access to the rivers is available to the public wishing to use the towpaths for walking as shown on Chart 50.

Towpath walking on the Lee

The Charts show all sections of towpath officially open to the public as chequered. Access may be obtained to many sections of towpath by the public but you are warned that these are not always intended as rights of way. Local notices may be displayed giving advice on this point.

The towpath between Limehouse and Bow alongside the Limehouse Cut is barred and locked for security reasons at Bow. You should not, therefore attempt walking from Limehouse, where access is possible via the Ship Lock gate in Narrow Street, without first obtaining permission and arranging to be met by the security staff at Bow who will unlock the gate for you.

Both this towpath and that from Bow to Old Ford Locks may be impassable on high spring tides due to flooding.

TIDAL INFORMATION

Bow Creek is fully tidal and is unnavigable at Low Water. High Tide reaches Bow Tidal Locks at about the same time as at London Bridge. When the flood tide reaches a level with the water in the Lee Navigation and Limehouse Cut the lock chambers are fully opened to allow craft free passage without having to wait for the locks to be worked in the normal manner. The level in the Navigation and the Limehouse Cut will, therefore, rise, affecting the level from the Limehouse Basin up to the tail of Old Ford Locks where High Water occurs about 3 minutes after that at Bow Locks. The tide also enters the Old River Lee and the Bow Back River (St Thomas's Creek). As the tide falls again, the locks at Bow are shut, but continue to be available for passage of craft by the normal lock-working method, for 2 hours after High Water. After this time it is unlikely that all but the very smallest craft would be able to reach the River Thames via Bow Creek.

In order to maintain the levels dictated by the opening and closing of Bow Locks, the Limehouse Ship Lock cannot be worked after High Water since the amount of water discharged by a working would seriously affect levels in the Limehouse Cut and the Lee Navigation below Old Ford due to the size of the lock and the amount of water required. Where the level in the River Thames rises to that within the Limehouse Basin, the ship lock will also be fully opened so that craft may proceed direct into the basin. Top and bottom gates will be closed, however, as soon as the ebb tide commences.

HERTFORD UNION CANAL
Prior notice of passage of the three locks on this canal may be given to the Regent's Section Inspector (01-790 3444) or contact may be made at Old Ford (Regent's) Lock (01-980 1426), or the Lock-keeper's offices at Bow or Old Ford (Lee) Locks, if assistance in working is required.

Bow Locks – River Lee Navigation

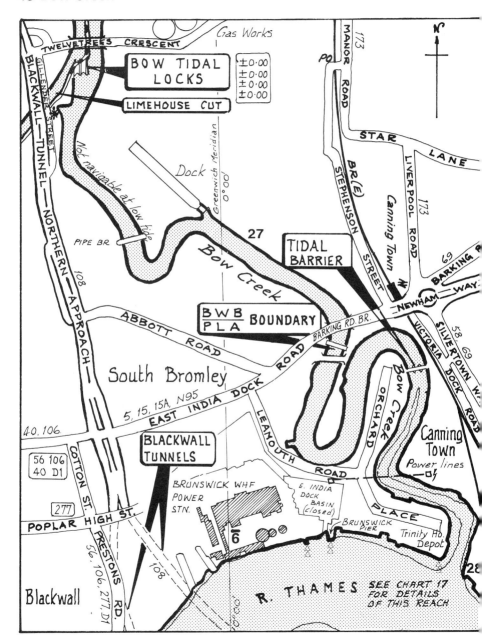

Tidal Constants on London Bridge		Mean Tidal Ranges		
HWS — 0hr 20m		Springs	21'6"	6.60m
LWS — 0hr 24m	at Bow Creek Mouth	in Thames navigation channel off creek		
HWN — 0hr 18m		Neaps	15'0"	4.60m
LWN — 0hr 29m		in Thames navigation channel off creek		

Duration of Rise and Fall of Average Spring and Neap Tides			
Flood		*Ebb*	
Springs	**Neaps**	**Springs**	**Neaps**
5hrs 45m.	6hrs 30m.	6hrs 30m.	6hrs 00m.

Ebb tide sets toward	
Reach	*Bank*
Bow Creek	Outsides of all bends.
Blackwall and Bugsby's Reaches to Victoria Entrance (now closed).	North Bank, thence hard into South Bank on bight to Woolwich Reach.

CHART DIRECTORY (Chart 48)

Port of London Authority
Assistant Harbour Master (Upper), Tower Pier, London, EC3N 4PL. (01-481 0720: if no reply call the Duty Officer on 01-855 0315) (VHF Channel 14)

Navigation Authority for Bow Creek from Thames to Barking Road Bridge.

British Waterways Board
Bow Locks, Bromley-by-Bow, London, E3. (01-987 5661)

Lock-keepers' Office at Tidal Locks. Locks worked only by keeper. All gates opened on high spring tides.

British Waterways Board
Security Force Office, Bow Locks, London, E3 (01-987 1321)

Installation Security.

Metropolitan Police
Thames Division, 98 High Street, Wapping, London, E1 9NE (01-488 5291) (VHF Channel 14 Call sign 'Thames Police')

Police Patrols in PLA Section, Creek Mouth to Barking Road Bridge.

(Shown on Chart 49)
The Rising Sun (*Inn*), 14 Gillender Street, E3 (01-987 3726)
The Queen Victoria (*Inn*), 1 Gillender Street, E3 (01-987 4525/3764)

Towpath *There is no towpath in Bow Creek*
Tidal Barrier Headroom: Undersides of gates when raised are 9.15m above MHWS.
Cill depths: East & Centre: 6.70m below MHWS
*   West   : 3.65m below MHWS*
Tidal range:(Springs): 6.50m approx.
Lights: displayed at top of each gantry.   2 Fixed horizontal orange = Passage permitted.
                            1 Flashing red = Barrier closed
Operating Authority: Thames Water Authority (Lea Division) (Waltham Cross 23611).

9 Bromley by Bow

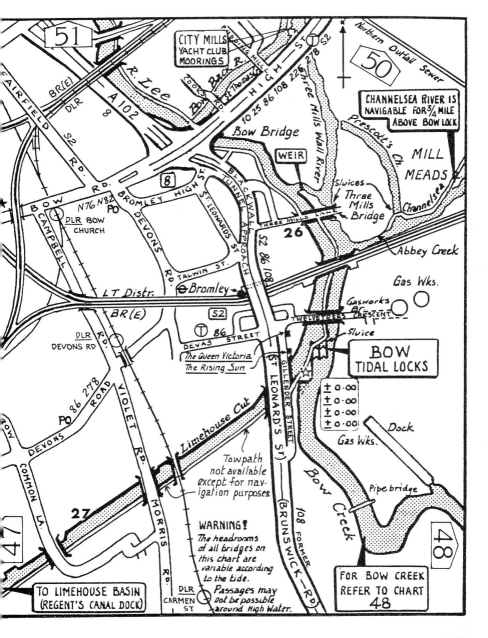

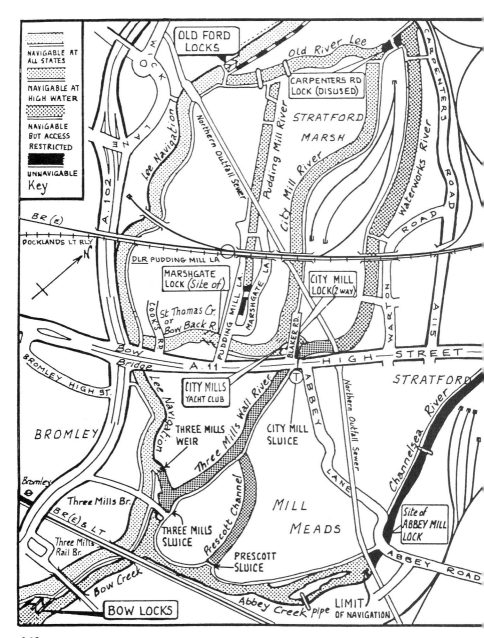

Old Ford

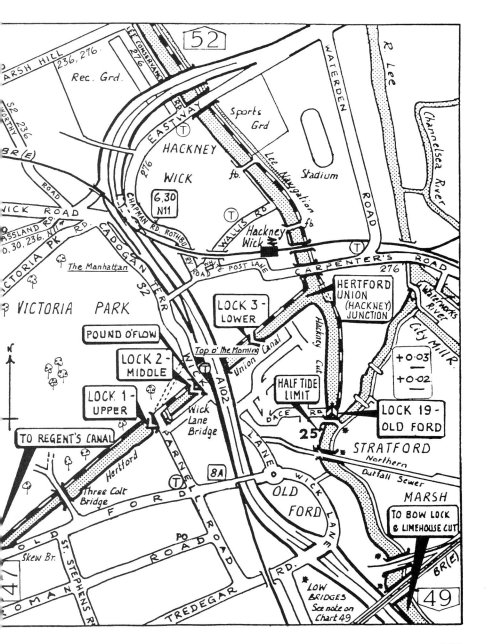

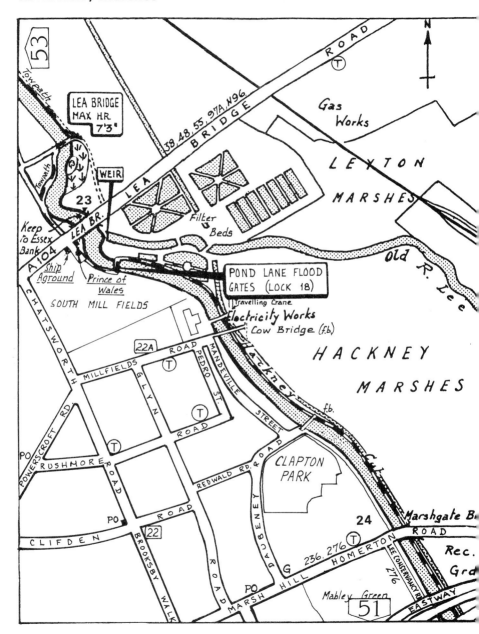

3 Warwick Reservoirs

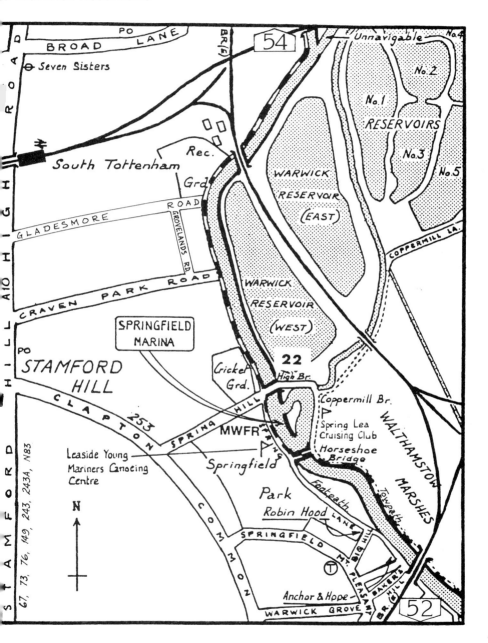

Lock rise (or fall)	Lock Name and No.		Falls from	Rises from
† Tidal – Level to 12'0" (Paired)	Bow Tidal Locks		Old Ford	Bow Creek
Pt. tidal (Paired)	Old Ford	(19)	Hertford	Bow Creek
4'0"	Hertford Union Lower	(3)	Regent's Canal	River Lee (Hackney Cut)
10'0"	Hertford Union Middle	(2)	Regent's Canal	River Lee (Hackney Cut)
8'0"	Hertford Union Upper	(1)	Regent's Canal	River Lee (Hackney Cut)
Nil	Pond Lane Flood Gates	(18)	Hertford*	Bow Creek*

*Only when in use. None of the Bow Back Rivers Locks is operable.
† Bow Locks worked by keepers. For times of working telephone 01-987 5661

CHART DIRECTORY (Charts 49 – 53)

For key to letter references see p. 21

49	**British Waterways Board** Bow Locks, Bromley-by-Bow, London, E3 (01-987 5661)	*Lock-keeper's Office at tidal locks.* Locks worked only by keeper. All gates opened on high spring tides.
49	**British Waterways Board** Security Force Office, Bow Locks, London, E3 (01-987 1321)	*Installation Security.*
49	**Metropolitan Police** 111 Bow Road, London, E3 (01-488 5212)	*Emergency calls only – Dial 999.*
51	**British Waterways Board** Old Ford Locks, Dace Road, London, E3 (01-985 4162)	*Lock-keeper's Office.* (W) Locks may be manually worked by boat crews when not attended.
51	**City Mills Yacht Club** Blaker Road, High Street, London, E15	*Club Moorings.*
51	**British Waterways Board** Hertford Union (Upper) Lock, Parnell Road, London. E3 (01-980 1946)*	*Lock-keeper's Office.* All three Hertford Union Locks worked by keeper or crews.
52	**British Waterways Board** Lea Bridge Weir, Lea Bridge Road, London, E5 (01-985 4876)	*Weir Keeper's Office.*

*If no reply phone 01-790 3444 to which prior notice of passage may be given.

52	**Springfield Marina**	*Boatyard.* (Lea Valley Regional
	Springhill, Upper Clapton, London, E5	Park Authority)
	(01-806 1717)	(B, D, M, R, U, W)

51	**Top of the Morning** *(Inn),* 129 Cadogan Terrace, London, E9 (01-985 1468)
51	**The Manhattan** *(Bar).* 69 Cadogan Terrace, London, E9 (01-985 6206)
52	**The Ship Aground** *(Inn)*, 144 Lea Bridge Road, London, E5 (01-985 5273)
52	**The Prince of Wales** *(Inn)*, 146 Lea Bridge Road, London, E5 (01-985 5735)
53	**The Robin Hood** *(Inn)*, High Hill Ferry, London, E5 (01-806 1720)
53	**The Anchor and Hope** *(Inn)*, 15 High Hill Ferry, London, E5 (01-806 1730)

River Lee by junction with Hertford Union Canal (Hackney Junction) *Photo: Derek Pratt*

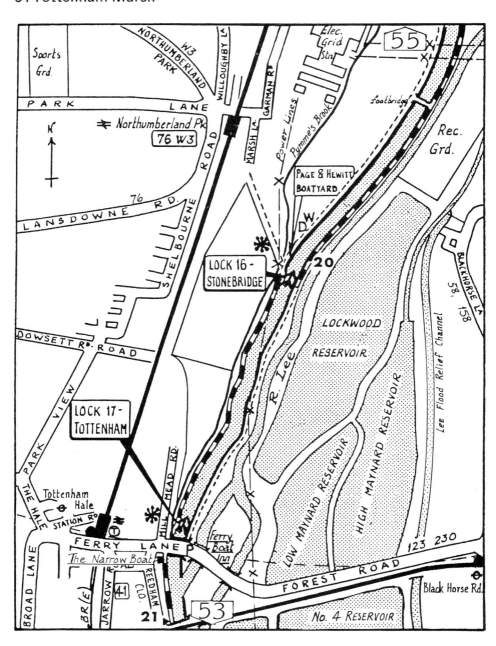

55 Edmonton

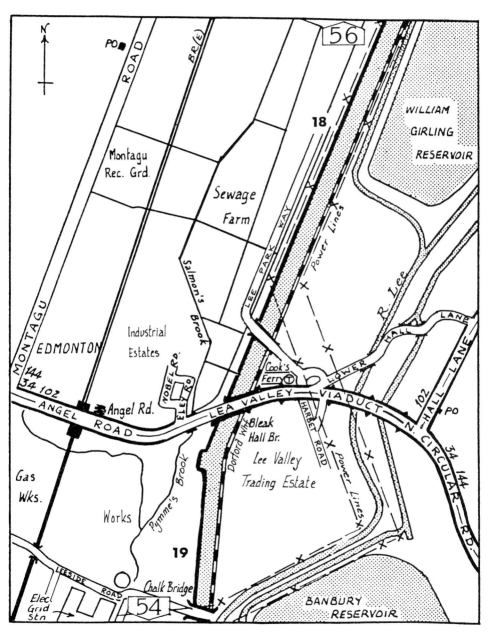

N

PO

ROAD

Be(E)

56

WILLIAM
GIRLING
RESERVOIR

18

Montagu
Rec. Grd.

Sewage
Farm

Lee Park Way

Power Lines

Salmon's Brook

R. Lee

HALL LANE

MONTAGU ROAD

EDMONTON

Industrial
Estates

144
34 102

NOBEL RD.

ELEY RD.

Cook's
Ferry

LOWER HALL

102

PO

ANGEL ROAD

Angel Rd.

LEA VALLEY VIADUCT

N. CIRCULAR RD.

34 144

Gas
Wks.

Pymme's Brook

Dorford W?

Bleak
Hall Br.

HARBET ROAD

Lee Valley
Trading Estate

Power Lines

Works

19

LEESIDE ROAD

Chalk Bridge

54

BANBURY
RESERVOIR

Elec
Grid
Stn

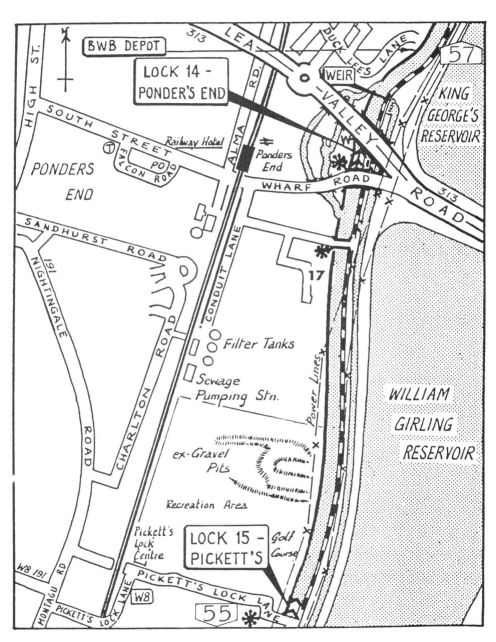

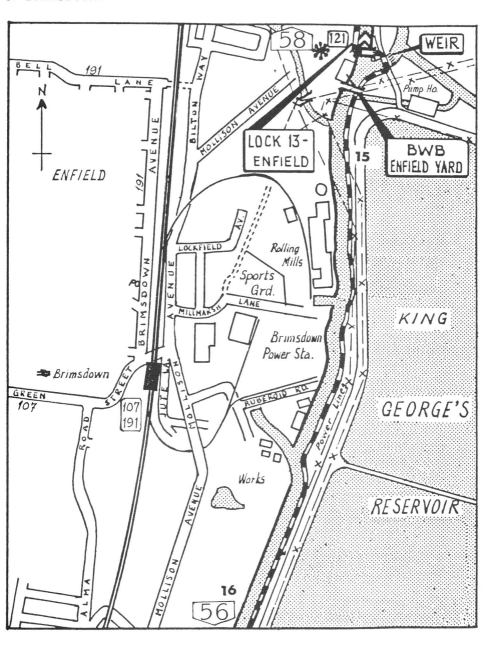

57 Brimsdown

ENFIELD

BELL LANE 191

N

191 AVENUE

BRIMSDOWN AVENUE

BILTON WAY

MOLLISON AVENUE

58

121

WEIR

Pump Ho.

LOCK 13 - ENFIELD

BWB ENFIELD YARD

15

AV. LOCKFIELD

Rolling Mills

Sports Grd.

MILLMARSH LANE

Brimsdown Power Sta.

KING

Brimsdown

GREEN 107

STREET

JUTE LA.

MOLLISON AVENUE

107 191

RUBEROID RD.

Power Lines

GEORGE'S

Works

RESERVOIR

ROAD

ALMA

MOLLISON AVENUE

16

56

Lock rise (or fall)	Lock Name and No.		Falls from	Rises from
7'6" Paired (Mech.)	Tottenham	(17)	Hertford	Bow Creek
7'6" Paired (Mech.)	Stonebridge	(16)	Hertford	Bow Creek
7'6" Single (Non-Mech.)	Pickett's	(15)	Hertford	Bow Creek
7'6" Paired (Mech.)	Ponder's End	(14)	Hertford	Bow Creek
10'0" Single (Hand)	Enfield	(13)	Hertford	Bow Creek
7'6" Single (Hand)	Rammey Marsh*	(12)	Hertford	Bow Creek
7'6" Single (Hand)	Waltham Town*	(11)	Hertford	Bow Creek

*Above Enfield lock dimensions reduce to 13'3" wide – Cill depth 4'9"
Locks 11–17 worked by boat crews. Locks 14–17 attended by keepers. For duty hours telephone Lea Valley 764626.

CHART DIRECTORY (Charts 54–58)

For key to letter references see p. 21

54 **British Waterways Board**
Tottenham Locks, Mill Mead Road,
Tottenham, N17 (01-808 3918)

Lock-keeper's Office.
(P) nearby.
Lock worked manually by boat crews when not attended.

Metropolitan Police
398 High Road, Tottenham, N17
(01-801 2151)

Emergency calls only – Dial 999

54 **British Waterways Board**
Stonebridge Locks, Marsh Lane,
Northumberland Park, N17
(01-808 4643)

Lock-keeper's Office.
Lock worked manually by boat crews when not attended.

54 **Page and Hewitt**
The Boathouse, Marsh Lane, Stonebridge
Locks, Northumberland Park N17
(01-808 9013)

Boatyard.
(B, C, D, E, G, H, M, R, U, W)

56 **British Waterways Board**
Pickett's Lock, Pickett's Lock Lane,
London, N9 (01-807 4650)

Lock-keeper's Office.
Lock worked manually by boat crews when not attended.

56 **British Waterways Board**
Ponder's End Locks, Lea Valley Road,
Ponder's End, Enfield, Middx
(01-804 1303).

Lock-keeper's Office.
(W)
Lock worked manually by boat crews when not attended.

56 **British Waterways Board**
Enfield Depot
Duck Lees Lane,
Ponders End, Mddx. (01-804 5552)

Freight Depot

Metropolitan Police
204 High Street, Ponder's End, Enfield,
Middx (01-367 2222)

Emergency calls only – Dial 999.

58 Enfield and Waltham

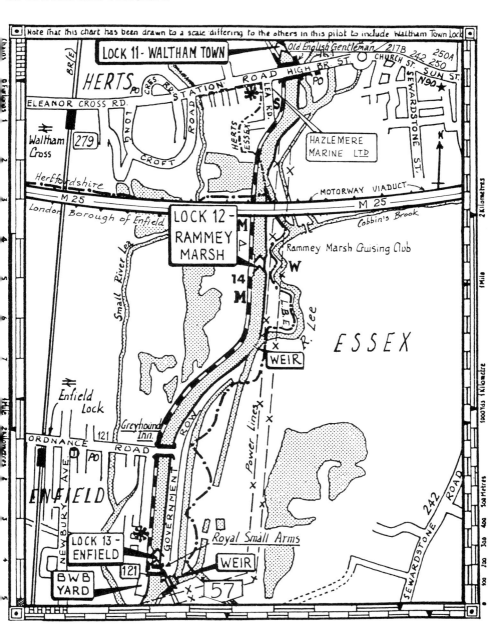

57	**British Waterways Board** Enfield Yard, Ordnance Road, Enfield Lock, Middx (Lea Valley 764626)	*Lee Section Inspector.*
57, 58	**British Waterways Board** Enfield Lock, Ordnance Road, Enfield Lock, Middx (Lea Valley 762110)	*Lock-keeper's Office.* Lock worked by boat crews.
58	**British Waterways Board** Newman's Weir, Enfield Lock, Middx (Lea Valley 762548)	*Weir Keeper.*
	Metropolitan Police 41 Baker Street, Enfield, Middx (01-367 2222)	*Emergency calls only – Dial 999*
58	**British Waterways Board** Rammey Marsh Lock, Waltham Cross, Herts. (Lea Valley 762831)	*Lock-keeper's Office.* (S, W) Lock worked by boat crews.
58	**British Waterways Board** Waltham Town Lock, High Bridge, Waltham Abbey, Essex	*Unattended lock.* Lock worked by boat crews.
58	**Metropolitan Police** 35 Sun Street, Waltham Abbey, Essex (Lea Valley 716222)	*Emergency calls only – Dial 999.*
58	**Hazlemere Marine Ltd** Highbridge Street, Waltham Abbey, Essex EN9 1BD (Lea Valley 711865/711333)	*Marina* (C, E, G, I, M, R, S, U, W)

54	**The Narrow Boat**, Reedham Close, N17 (01-808 4187)
54	**Ferry Boat Inn**, Ferry Lane, London, N17 (01-808 4631).
55	**Cook's Ferry Inn**, Angel Road, London, N18 (01-807 5115).
56	**Railway Hotel**, South Street, Ponder's End, Enfield, Middx (01-804 1513).
58	**Royal Small Arms** (*Inn*), Ordnance Road, Enfield Lock, Middx (Lea Valley 764749).
58	**Greyhound Inn,** 425 Ordnance Road, Enfield Lock, Middx (Lea Valley 764612).
58	**Old English Gentleman** (*Inn*), Highbridge St, Waltham Abbey, Essex (Waltham Cross 22634).

Public Towpath Tottenham Locks to Waltham
Access Points   Ferry Boat Inn, Tottenham
                    Stonebridge Locks
                    Cook's Ferry Inn, off Lea Valley Viaduct
                    Pickett's Lock
                    Wharf Road
                    Ponder's End Locks
                    Enfield Lock
                    Ordnance Road
                    High Bridge, Waltham

For continuation North – See O.S. Nicholson's Guide to the Waterways, Volume 1 – South.

PUBLIC TRANSPORT SERVICES

Railway Services

Station	Region or line	Route	*Normal Frequency
Canning Town	MR	Richmond – N. Woolwich	20 mins
Bromley-by-Bow	LT	District/Metropolitan**	5 mins
Hackney Wick	MR	Richmond – N. Woolwich	20 mins
Clapton	ER	Liverpool Street – Chingford	20 mins
South Tottenham	ER	Kentish Town – Barking	60 mins
Seven Sisters	ER	Liverpool St – Enfield Town	20 mins
	LT	Victoria Line	4/8 mins
Tottenham Hale	ER	Liverpool St – Bishops Stortford	30 mins
	LT	Victoria Line	10 mins
Black Horse Rd	ER	Kentish Town – Barking	60 mins
	LT	Victoria Line	10 mins
Northumberland Park	ER	Liverpool St – Bishops Stortford	30 mins
Angel Road	ER	Liverpool St – Bishops Stortford	30 mins
Ponder's End	ER	Liverpool St – Bishops Stortford	30 mins
Brimsdown	ER	Liverpool St – Bishops Stortford	30 mins
Enfield Lock	ER	Liverpool St – Bishops Stortford	30 mins
Waltham Cross	ER	Liverpool St – Bishops Stortford	30 mins

*Not necessarily on Sundays or at 'off-peak' times.
**Metropolitan Line trains at peak times only. Change at Whitechapel.

Docklands Light Railway (opening Summer 1987)

Stations: Carmen Street, Devons Road, Bow Church, Pudding Mill Lane.
(not charted): Poplar, All Saints, Stratford.

Phase One of the DLR will run from Tower Gateway to Stratford via Poplar or to Island Gardens at Saunders Ness via Canary Wharf and between Island Gardens and Stratford.
Further information from LDDC (01-515 3000).

London Bus Services

Bus route numbers are shown along principal main roads shown on the charts. Bus route terminals are shown with the route number boxed.

Route No.	Termini	Route No.	Termini
5	Becontree Heath, Old Street and Waterloo	41	Archway Station, Tottenham Hale and Ferry Lane Estate
6	Kensal Rise Station and Hackney Wick		
8	Bow church and Willesden	48	London Bridge and Walthamstow Central Station
8a	Old Ford and London Bridge Station	55	Victoria Station and Whipps Cross
10	Victoria and Wanstead	56	Aldgate, Poplar and West Ham Garage
15	East Ham and Ladbroke Grove	58	North Woolwich, Canning Town and Walthamstow
15a	East Ham and Ladbroke Grove		
22	Putney Common and Homerton	67	Wood Green and Aldgate
22a	Clapton Park and Wapping	69	North Woolwich and Chingford
25	Ilford and Victoria Station	73	Hammersmith, Stoke Newington and Tottenham Garage
30	Hackney Wick and Putney Heath		
34	Barnet and Whipps Cross	76	Northumberland Park Station, Tottenham Garage, Moorgate and Victoria
38	Victoria Station and Leyton Green		
40	Herne Hill and Poplar	86	Romford, Stratford, Limehouse, Mile End

Route No.	Termini	Route No.	Termini
97a	Chingford Station, Walthamstow Central Station and Hackney Central or Leyton Green	243a	Wood Green and Liverpool Street Station
		250	Waltham Cross, Loughton Station and South Woodford
102	Golders Green and Chingford	250a	Waltham Cross and Upshire
106	Finsbury Park, Poplar and Isle of Dogs	276	East Beckton District Centre, Hackney Wick and Stoke Newington
107	Brimsdown Station and Queensbury Station	277	Poplar, Angel and Smithfield
108	Stratford and Eltham	278	North Woolwich and Limehouse
121	Turnpike Lane Station and Enfield Lock	313	Chingford Station and Potters Bar (London Country)
123	Winchmore Hill and Ilford Station		
144	Ilford Station and Turnpike Lane	S2	Stratford and Clapton (Sat & Sun to Lee Valley Ice Centre)
149	Ponders End, Liverpool Street and Waterloo	W3	Finsbury Park and Northumberland Park Station
158	Stratford and Chingford Mount		
173	Stratford and Becontree Heath	W8	Chase Farm Hospital and Picketts Lock Centre
191	Brimsdown Station, Enfield and Lower Edmonton Station	D1	Mile End Station and Poplar (Docklands Clipper
217b	Enfield, Waltham Cross and Upshire	**All-Night Bus Services**	
225	Aldgate, Becontree Heath and Dagenham	N76	Victoria Station and Wanstead Station
230	Leytonstone and Finsbury Park	N83	Trafalgar Square and Wood Green
236	Leytonstone and Finsbury Park	N90	Victoria and Hammond Street
242	Chingford Station and Potters Bar Station	N95	Victoria and Dagenham
243	Wood Green and Holborn Circus	N96	Waterloo and Chingford Station

River Lee — Pond Lane flood gates near Lea Bridge *Photo: Derek Pratt*

Part IV
River Thames
The Tideway from Bow Creek
to Sea Reach

Looking back at the Thames Barrier - view downstream

Section 9 River Thames —
Bow Creek to Sea Reach

GENERAL

Distance	43½ statute land miles (Bow Creek Mouth to Sea Reach No. 1 Buoy).
No. of locks	Nil
Tunnels	None
Bridges	1 Proposed 72 metres east of Dartford Tunnel (Opening 1992).
Headroom	250 ft (76.20 m) (Electric power cables). 177 ft (54 m) when Dartford Bridge completed.
Branches	Bow Creek (to a point just downstream of Barking Road Bridge — See Sections 4 and 8 of this guide). Barking Creek (See Chart 59). Dartford Creek (See Chart 60). Holehaven Creek (See Chart 62). Benfleet Creek (See Chart 63).

Maximum Dimensions	*Length*	Unlimited
	Beam	Unlimited
	Draught	Bow Creek to Margaret Ness 6 metres at MLWS
		Margaret Ness to Dagenham 7 - 8 metres at MLWS (minimum of 6 metres off Barking)
		Dagenham to Mucking Flats 8 - 10 metres at MLWS (minimum of 7½ metres off Denton)
		Mucking Flats to Sea Reach No. 1 9 - 11 metres at MLWS

The above measurements of draught apply to the dredged channel delineated on the chart by pecked lines. Small craft are asked to avoid using this channel, which is obviously designed for commercial shipping. A continuous contour of 5 metres is shown on the chart as well as the point of MLWS denoted by a dotted line. There is a mean tidal range of 5½ - 6 metres at Tilbury which may be taken as an average for the six charts. MLWN average 1¼ metres above MLWS.

The tide ebbs at up to 3 knots during Springs (about 2 hours after HW at Tilbury) and up to 2 knots during Neaps (at the same point and time). Rates of flow on the flood and at other times on the ebb are slower.

Up to date information should always be obtained from the PLA Hydrographic Officer or the Assistant Harbour Master.

All tidal constants shown on these charts are based on London Bridge.

Waterway Authority for navigation

The Port of London Authority, Europe House, World Trade Centre, London, E1 9AA (01-481 8484)

Harbour Master, Port of London Authority, Thames House, St Andrews Road, Tilbury, Essex, RM18 7JH (Tilbury (03752) 3444).

Assistant Harbour Master (Upper) Teddington to Crayford Ness; Thames Navigation Service, Tower Pier, London, EC3N 4PL (Tel: 01-481 0720).

Assistant Harbour Master (Lower) Crayford Ness to Sea Reach No. 1 Buoy; Thames Navigation Service, Royal Terrace Pier Road, Gravesend, Kent DA12 2BG (Tel: Gravesend (0474) 67684).

Licensing A licence to navigate the tidal Thames is not required.

COMMUNICATIONS

Shipping approaching or leaving the Thames may obtain navigational and tidal information by the following means:

Area	*Radio	Telephone	Radar Coverage
Erith to Estuary *Charts 60 to 64*	'GRAVESEND RADIO' VHF Ch 12, 16, 18, 20	Gravesend (0474) 60311	Erith to Southend and Estuary
London Bridge to Erith and Woolwich Barrier *Charts 59 & 60*	'WOOLWICH RADIO' or 'BARRIER CONTROL' VHF Ch 74, 16, 22	01-855 0315	London Bridge to Erith
River Medway Approach *Chart 64*	MEDWAY RADIO VHF Ch 14, 16, 22	Sheerness 663025	River Medway and approaches

*The first quoted channel in each case is the normal working frequency.
The call-sign for each station is that given in the 'Radio' column.
Thames Navigation Service patrol craft operate on VHF Channels 12, 14, 16 & 6. Call sign 'Thames Patrol'.
Ship/Tug communications are normally conducted on VHF Channels 6, 8 and 10 in the Thames and on 6 and 9 in the Medway.

Way Points

Clearance of passage is not normally required for small craft under 50 g.r.t. The way points for reporting, however, have been shown on the charts. The figure in the way point circle is the VHF Channel on which the report should be made.

Introduction to the Lower Sections

Considerable commercial traffic is encountered in the Thames below Woolwich and pleasure craft must be navigated so that no risk of collision or hindrance is offered to such traffic. Furthermore the author does not recommend the navigation of a craft solely designed for inland waterway cruising, either by virtue of its hull design or by virtue of its lack of power.

Information is therefore offered in this Section and the Appendices I, II and III to those who have the proper equipment for exploring the lower reaches of the Thames, or for those visiting the Thames who may wish to enter the inland waterways network at one of the points of entry described elsewhere in this guide. These appendices are not intended to be exhaustive, neither can any responsibility be accepted for errors of fact, omission or detail and would-be navigators are strongly recommended to acquire the larger-scale charts published by the Admiralty, the serial numbers of which are noted on page 203 (Appendix II). Any errors noted by readers, or comments which would assist the publishers in a revision of this section, would be welcomed.

Rules of the River

Please read the Directions in Appendix I on page 201. Reference should be made to the Practical Navigation notes on page 12 and notice should be taken that for the purposes of these appendices the *Fairway* is further defined in addition to the meaning in Appendix I as:
- a) the 1,000 ft wide channel from No. 1 Sea Reach Buoy to Gravesend and the main navigational channel from Gravesend to London Bridge, as indicated on the Authority's and Admiralty charts,
- b) the normal approach to the deep-water anchorages of the Warp and Southend-on-Sea.

Below London Bridge, craft of less than 20 metres in length shall not hamper the passage of a vessel which can only navigate inside the fairway.

Craft and vessels shall not enter into nor cross the fairway between No. 1 Sea Reach Buoy and London Bridge so as to obstruct another vessel proceeding along the fairway.

Keep clear of vessels and tugs about to berth or moor.

No vessel at any time, in fog or in clear visibility, shall anchor in the fairway except in emergency or for the purpose of manoeuvring.

Vessels in doubt that sufficient action is being taken to avoid collision may indicate, by sounding five or more short and rapid blasts on the whistle.

In times of fog you must not:

unless equipped with *and operating* radar, navigate in the fairway unless it is for the purpose of navigating out of the fairway.

bring up nor anchor within the fairway.

Small craft are warned that commercial vessels equipped with radar do navigate in fog and poor visibility.

Copies of the PLA Byelaws are obtainable from the address given at the head of page 180.

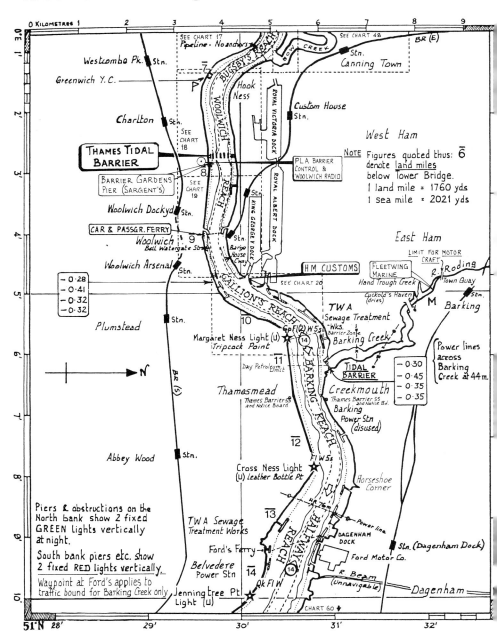

Tidal Constants on London Bridge		Mean Tidal Ranges	
HWS — 0 hr 30m		Springs	20'6"
LWS — 0 hr 45m	at Barking Creek		6.25m
HWN — 0 hr 35m		Neaps	14'6"
LWN — 0 hr 35m			4.42m

Duration of Rise and Fall of Average Spring and Neap Tides

Flood		*Ebb*	
Springs	**Neaps**	**Springs**	**Neaps**
6 hrs 00m	6 hrs 30m	6 hrs 10m	5 hrs 50m

Ebb tide sets toward

Bugsby's Reach	South Bank
Woolwich Reach	None
Note. Tidal set below Woolwich is variable on both	*See individual*
flood and ebb and considerable cross-currents	*notes attached*
and eddies are set up in the neighbourhood of	*to respective*
jetties and piers as well as off promontories.	*charts.*

Light Structures	Characteristics	Distance	Height
Margaret Ness (Tripcock Point)	Gp Fl(2) 5 sec	8M	11m
Cross Ness (Leather Bottle Point)	Fl 5 sec	5M	6m
Jenningtree Point	Qk Fl	5M	11m

CHART DIRECTORY

For key to letter references see p. 21

For details of services upstream of Margaret Ness please turn to pages 78 and 82.

BARKING CREEK AND RIVER RODING

Distance   Barking Creek 1²/₃ statute land miles ⎫ Navigable section
River Roding 1³/₄ statute land miles ⎭

Number of locks   1 (Tidal doors)
Tunnels   Nil
Bridges   4 + 1 Tidal barrier (see below)
Branches   4 (to wharves)
Head of navigation   Ilford Bridge (Town Quay for motor craft)
Maximum dimensions of craft proceeding to Ilford Bridge on MHWS

Length	87'6" (26.7m)
Beam	16'9" (5.1m)
Draught	5'0" (1.5m)
Headroom	7'6" (2.3m) *Maximum Headroom in Barking Creek* 28'6" (8.7m)

Tidal Barrier Dimensions:

Width:	125'0" (38.1m)
Draught:	23'9" (7.23m) at MHWS
Headroom:	107'6" (32.77m) at MHWS
Operating Authority:	Thames Water Authority

Tidal constants *See chart.* (High water at Ilford Bridge, as London Br.) This waterway is tidal throughout, although the River Roding section used to be maintained to a navigable depth by the operation of the tidal doors at Barking. Craft could only pass into the Roding when the tide in the creek made a level with the river and the tidal doors could be opened. The tidal doors have now been dismantled and navigation can only be conducted above this point on high tides.

Fleetwing Marine	*Moorings, Chandlery*
50, Zeta Wharf, Abbey Road, Barking, Essex IG11 7BT	C, D, E, G, M, P, R, W
(01-594 3704)	

Barking Creek is under the jurisdiction of the Port of London Authority. The River Roding is under the nominal authority of the Barking and Ilford Navigation Co (1961) Ltd, whose agents are Messrs Younghusband Stephens & Co Ltd, London Road, Barking, Essex. (Tel: 01-594 3467)

Piers 8 and 9 and Control Tower, Thames Barrier, Woolwich

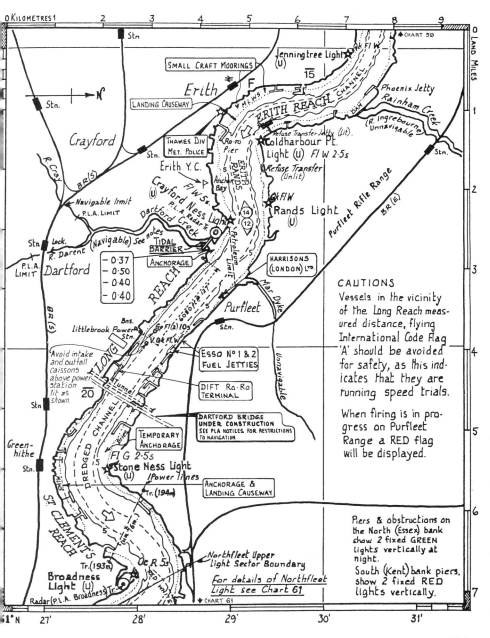

CAUTIONS

Vessels in the vicinity of the Long Reach measured distance, flying International Code flag 'A' should be avoided for safety, as this indicates that they are running speed trials.

When firing is in progress on Purfleet Range a RED flag will be displayed.

Piers & obstructions on the North (Essex) bank show 2 fixed GREEN lights vertically at night.

South (Kent) bank piers, show 2 fixed RED lights vertically.

For details of Northfleet Light see Chart 61

Tidal Constants on London Bridge		Mean Tidal Ranges	
HWS — 0 hr 37m		Springs	23'0"
LWS — 0 hr 50m	at Purfleet		7.00m
HWN — 0 hr 40m		Neaps	15'6"
LWN — 0 hr 40m			4.80m

Duration of Rise and Fall of Average Spring and Neap Tides

Flood		Ebb	
Springs	**Neaps**	**Springs**	**Neaps**
6 hrs 00m	6 hrs 25m	6 hrs 15m	5 hrs 55m

Light Structures	Characteristics	Distance	Height
Jenningtree Point	Qk Fl	5M	11m
Coldharbour Point	Fl 2.5 sec	8M	11m
Rands	Qk Fl	7M	6m
Crayford Ness	Fl 5 sec and F	14M & 3M	16m
Stone Ness	Fl G 2.5 sec and FG	9M & 3M	13m
Broadness	Oc R 5s	12M	12m

CHART DIRECTORY

Port of London Authority
Causeway, Erith, Kent

Not permanently manned.

Thames Division Metropolitan Police
Controlled from Wapping
(01-488 5291)

Launch patrols
In emergency dial 999.
(Metropolitan Police launches
patrol downstream to Dartford
Creek.)

Erith Yacht Club
Club Ship 'Folgefonn', Anchor Bay, Erith,
Kent.

Visitors' moorings by arrangement.

West Street Service Station
West Street, Erith, Kent (Erith 37348)

Fuel
(Landing at Erith Causeway)

Esso Petroleum Co. Ltd
Thames Installation, Purfleet, Essex (Purfleet 5841)

Fuel. (Metered supplies)
Diesel and gas oil (24 hours)
Subject to jetties not being
occupied.

H. A. Cross
82 London Road, Stone, Dartford, Kent
(Dartford 20789)

Calor gas agents.
(Land at Greenhithe)

DARTFORD AND CRAYFORD NAVIGATION (Dartford Creek)

Distance	River Darent 2¾ statute land miles ⎱ Navigable sections
	River Cray ¾ statute land mile ⎰
Number of locks	1 (At Dartford) *not in service*
Tunnels	Nil
Bridges	3 including tidal barrier (see below)
Branches	River Cray is a branch of the Darent.
Head of navigation	River Darent: Dartford Rail Bridge
	River Cray: Crayford Sawmills

Maximum dimensions of craft proceeding to Dartford:

Length	165'0" (50.3m)
Beam	23'0" (7.0m)
Draught	7'0" (rising to about 11'0" on High Tides) (2.13 − 3.35m)
	6'0" (1.8m) in River Cray and beyond Dartford wharves.
Headroom	29'0" (8.83m)

Tidal Barrier dimensions:

Width:	98'6" (30m)
Draught:	6'3" (2m) rising
Headroom:	40'0" (12.2m) (at MHWS)

Operating authority:
Southern Water Authority (Kent Division)

Towing path   Bradshaw and Edwards both state that there is none; however there is a linear footpath following the east bank of the River Darent from Dartford (Mill Pond Road) to the Thames and a linear footpath following the west bank from Crayford Mill on the Cray to the confluence with the Darent and thence to the Thames and Crayford Ness Light.

For navigational purposes throughout the authority is the Dartford and Crayford Navigation Commissioners, Dartford Locks, Dartford, Kent. (Dartford 24039).

Tidal constants	*Dartford Creek Mouth*	*Dartford Locks*
High Water Springs	− 0hr 37m	−0hr 33 m
Low Water Springs	− 0hr 50m	−0hr 45 m
High Water Neaps	− 0hr 40m	−0hr 35 m
Low Water Neaps	− 0hr 40m	−0hr 35 m

There are no pleasure craft facilities on either branch of the navigation, which was of a purely commercial nature. There is barely any traffic left and the future of the navigation is uncertain.

NAVIGATION NOTES Jenningtree to Broad Ness

The main flood sets hard off Coldharbour Point towards Erith town. Craft coming upstream on the flood should keep to north shore. Up to an hour after flood commences an extreme contra-flood eddy sets in from below Erith town as far down as Crayford Ness. Over this same area the ebb runs very strongly up to 4 knots at equinoctial springs. Keep clear of the Littlebrook Power Station intake and outfall caissons which are shown on the chart and are specially lit at night.

Ebb tides set fairly rapidly into the bight at Greenhithe and on the flood eddies set in along the Greenhithe shore.

Northfleet Hope reach is unsuitable for anchoring. Thurrock Yacht Clubhouse can be reached by dinghy, if you are able to moor or anchor off. South shore of the reach is dangerous, due to ebb set towards the shore and lack of suitable holding ground.

Particular care should be exercised in this reach due to the strong currents and large vessels manoeuvring for berths.

Landings can be made at Erith Causeway for shops, telephone, rail station and pub; Greenhithe Causeway for telephone, pub and repairs and Thurrock Y.C. as above for shops and rail station.

Dartford Bridge (proposed)
Construction work may start soon after publication of this guide. Special instructions to shipping in connection with the works will be given in PLA Notices to Mariners obtainable from the PLA Harbourmaster's Office at Tilbury. Information can also be obtained from TNS Gravesend (0474) 60311 or on VHF Channel 12.

Tidal Constants on London Bridge		Mean Tidal Ranges	
HWS — 0 hr 59m		Springs	22'3"
LWS — 1 hr 20m	at Tilbury		6.80m
HWN — 0 hr 45m		Neaps	15'6"
LWN — 0 hr 45m			4.80m

Duration of Rise and Fall of Average Spring and Neap Tides			
Flood		Ebb	
Springs	Neaps	Springs	Neaps
6 hrs 00m	6 hrs 25m	6 hrs 15m	5 hrs 55m

Light Structures	Characteristics	Distance	Height
Northfleet Upper	Occ WRG 10 sec R 126°–149° : W 149°–159° : G 159°–269° : W 269°–279°	12M–16M	30m
Northfleet Lower	Occ WR 5 sec W 164°–271° : R 271°–Shore	14M–17M	16m
Shornmead	Gp Fl(2) WRG 10 sec G Shore–80° : R 80°–85° : W 85°–88° : G 88°–141° : W 141°–205° : R 205°–213°	13M–17M	—

◖ Northfleet to Mucking Flats

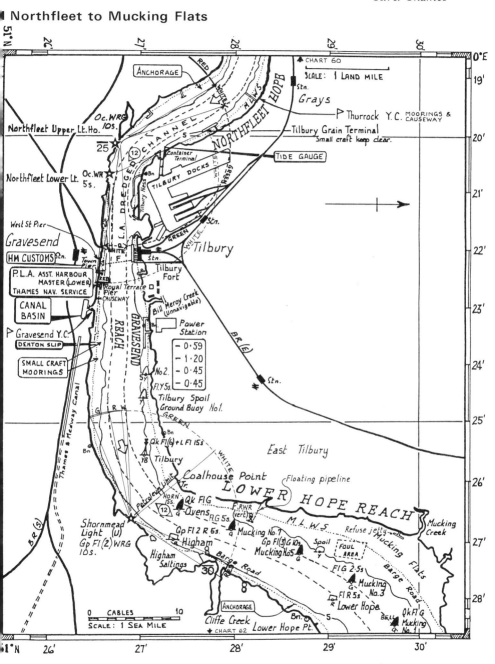

CHART DIRECTORY

Port of London Authority
Assistant Harbour Master (Lower), Thames
Navigation Centre, Royal Terrace Pier Road, Gravesend,
Kent DA12 2BG (Gravesend (0474) 67684)
Duty Officer, Thames Navigation Service
(Gravesend (0474) 57724) (24 hrs.)

Navigation Authority
Information on tides, moorings,
etc.
(For VHF Radio contact see page
180 under 'GRAVESEND
RADIO')

HM Customs
Gravesend (0474) 63555/60529 (Ext.29)
Tilbury (03752) 4121 (Ext.53)

General enquiries and clearance.
It may be necessary to land to
obtain clearance.

Port of London Health Authority
Denton Hospital or Denton Quarantine Station,
Gravesend, Kent (Day: Gravesend 63033
After hours: Tilbury (03752) 2663)

Medical Officer

Police
North Bank (Essex Police)
Grays Thurrock 77211
Tilbury 2541
(PLA) Tilbury 4714
South Bank (Kent County Constabulary)
Swanley, London Road. Gravesend 64451
Gravesend. Gravesend 64346

(In emergency – dial 999)

Port of London Authority
London Cruise Terminal (Tilbury Landing Stage)
(Tilbury (03752) 79194)

Landing only for railway station.

Thurrock Yacht Club
The Beach, Grays, Essex (Grays Thurrock (0375)
73720)

Moorings.

Gravesend Sailing Club
Promenade East, Gravesend, Kent (Gravesend 52392)

Moorings, Water

The Canal Basin
Gravesham Borough Council, Civic Centre,
Gravesend DA12 1AU
(Lock-keeper's office: Gravesend 52392)

Moorings
(Entrance to basin can be made
from 2 hours before High Water,
only manned at this time)

Domindus Ltd
2 Vale Road, Northfleet, Gravesend, Kent
(Gravesend 52763/65815/61250)

Small craft sales, chandlery

Gravesend Crescent Trading Ltd
Norfolk Road, Gravesend, Kent
(Gravesend 64855)

Calor Gas

Miller Marine Services
1a Terrace Street, Gravesend, Kent
(Gravesend 52287)

Chandlers

J. and R. Starbuck
73–75 West Street, Gravesend DA11 0BU
(Gravesend 3182)

Chandlers

Clifton Slipways
1 Clifton Parade, Gravesend, Kent
(Gravesend 64868)

Marine Engineers

E. W. Lewis
1 Victoria Avenue, Gravesend, Kent
(Gravesend 62000)

Marine Engineers

Motivators Ltd
Denton Slipway, Gravesend, Kent
(Gravesend 67881)

Marine Engineers

J. Collis Ltd (Ironmongers)
King Street, Gravesend, Kent
(Gravesend 2283)

Calor Gas stockist

Barking Creek Tidal Barrier nearing completion in 1982

62 Mucking Flats to Canvey Island

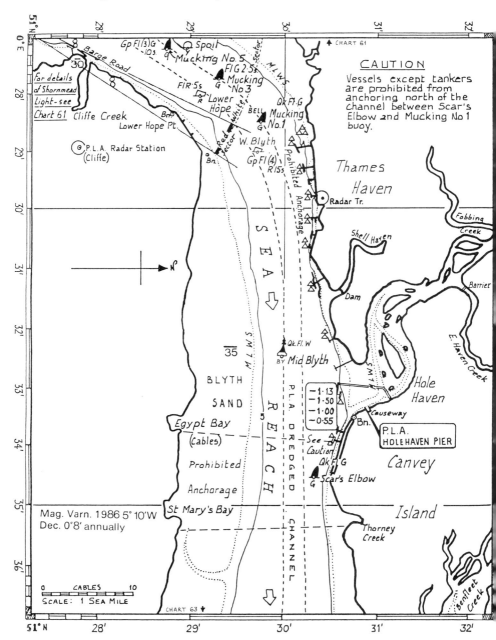

CAUTION

Vessels except tankers are prohibited from anchoring north of the channel between Scar's Elbow and Mucking No 1 buoy.

Mag. Varn. 1986 5°10'W
Dec. 0°8' annually

Tidal Constants on London Bridge		Mean Tidal Ranges	
HWS — 1 hr 13m		Springs	21'6"
LWS — 1 hr 50m	at Holehaven Entrance		6.60m
HWN — 1 hr 00m		Neaps	14'9"
LWN — 0 hr 55m			4.50m

Duration of Rise and Fall of Average Spring and Neap Tides			
Flood		*Ebb*	
Springs	**Neaps**	**Springs**	**Neaps**
6 hrs 00m	6 hrs 20m	6 hrs 15m	6 hrs 10m

CHART DIRECTORY

Port of London Authority
Piermaster, Holehaven Pier, Canvey Island, Essex
(Canvey Island (0268 68) 3041)

Limited moorings and information when manned

H.M. Customs
Shell Haven, Essex
(Stanford-le-Hope (0375) 671177)

Customs inspection
(Not normally suitable for small craft)

NAVIGATION NOTES

Gravesend Reach Small craft should avoid the Tilbury side although a landing may be made with caution at Tilbury Landing Stage by permission of the piermaster (Tilbury 79194) in order to reach the railway station. Anchorage is possible on the south shore half a mile below Gravesend Town Pier. There is also a landing point at the causeway 300m upstream of the Canal Basin from which all facilities can easily be reached.

Lower Hope Reach Keep to the south shore on the ebb tide and to the north shore on the flood but note that there is no inshore passage due to the floating pipe line from the "Voorbure" unit north of Mucking No 7 buoy. Avoid anchoring too close to Lower Hope Point as small vessels tend to cut rather close to the point if they are not required to stay in the dredged channel. Note that anchoring off the north (Thames Haven) shore is prohibited except for tankers.

Sea Reach Anchorage is available at Holehaven, but prior enquiry is advisable. Landing can be made at the PLA causeway off Lobster Smack stairs. Anchor off the west side of the fairway into the creek as the Canvey side is strewn with rubble which is uncovered at low tide. Note the cautions on the chart regarding cables and prohibited anchorage areas.

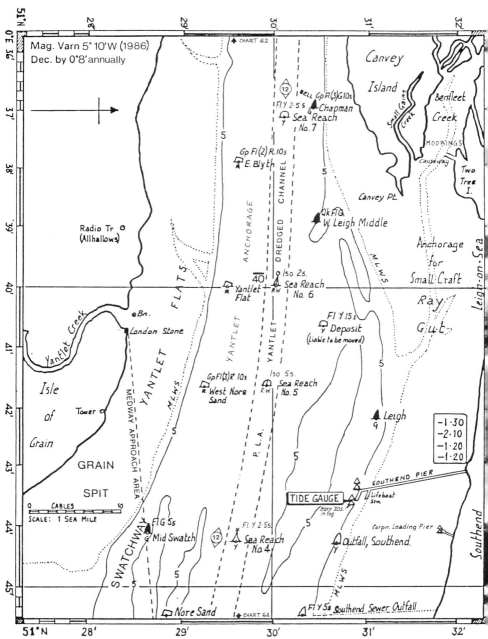

Tidal Constants on London Bridge		Mean Tidal Ranges	
HWS — 1 hr 30m ⎤		Springs	20'6"
LWS — 2 hr 10m ⎟ at Southend			6.20m
HWN — 1 hr 20m ⎟		Neaps	13'6"
LWN — 1 hr 20m ⎦			4.20m

Duration of Rise and Fall of Average Spring and Neap Tides

Flood		*Ebb*	
Springs	**Neaps**	**Springs**	**Neaps**
6 hrs 00m	6 hrs 20m	6 hrs 15m	6 hrs 15m

CHART DIRECTORY

Southend Pier
(Southend 355620)

Mooring enquiries, Information, Water

Foreshore Inspector
Bell Wharf Office, Leigh-on-Sea, Essex
(Southend (0702) 710561)
Pier Hill, Southend-on-Sea, Essex
(Southend 611889)

Mooring enquiries, Information

H.M. Coastguard
Maplin Way, Thorpe Bay, Southend-on-Sea,
Essex (Shoeburyness (03708) 4998)
Frinton Maritime Rescue Sub Centre
(Frinton (02556) 5518)

In emergency, dial 999 and ask
for 'Coastguard'

H.M. Customs
Southend Airport, Southend-on-Sea, Essex SS2 6YB
(Southend (0702) 547141)

Island Yacht Club
10, Wall Road, Canvey Island, Essex
(Canvey Island 683729)

Moorings in Small Gains Creek

Benfleet Yacht Club
Canvey Road, Canvey Island, Essex, SS8 0QT
(South Benfleet 2278)

Moorings in Benfleet Creek

Essex Yacht Club
Bembridge, Leigh-on-Sea, Essex (Southend 78404)

Moorings

Leigh-on-Sea Sailing Club
The Old Town, Leigh-on-Sea, Essex (Southend 76788)

Moorings

The Dauntless Company
The Bridge, Canvey Island (South Benfleet 3782)

Boatbuilders, Marine Engineers, Fuel, Gas, in Benfleet Creek

Halcon Marine
The Point, Canvey Island, Essex
(Canvey Island 685001)

Moorings, Slipping, Repairs

Dolphin Marine Engineering Ltd
17–18 High Street, Old Town, Leigh-on-Sea, Essex
(Southend 74627)

Marine engineers

Calor Gas Ltd Sales and Service
85, High Road, Benfleet (South Benfleet 2271)

Calor Gas

Johnson, Sons and Jago Ltd
Leigh-on-Sea, Essex (Southend 76639)

*Chandlery, Boatbuilding,
Marine engineers, Fuel, Gas.*

Mike's Boatyard Ltd
8 High Street, Old Town, Leigh-on-Sea, Essex
(Southend 713151)

*Chandlers, Boatbuilders, Marine
engineers, Gas, Electrical repairs.*

Southend Engineering Co
61 High Street, Old Town, Leigh-on-Sea, Essex
(Southend 78803)

Marine engineers

Walker Enterprises
West Street, Leigh-on-Sea, Essex (Southend 715677)

Boat Builders, Repairers

J. W. Davis and Son (Yachting) Ltd
5–6 Palmeira Arches, Westcliff-on-Sea, Essex
(Southend 346132)

Chandlers

Boatacs Ltd
142, Eastern Espl., Southend, Essex
(Southend 614777)
811 London Road, Westcliff-on-Sea, Essex
(Southend 75057)

*Chandlers
Riggers*

Shoreline (Yachtsman) Ltd
36 Eastern Esplanade, Southend-on-Sea, Essex
(Southend 68574/615678)

Chandlers

Sail America
Calvia Works, Prince Avenue, Southend-on-Sea,
Essex (Southend 335536)

Boat and small craft sales

Elmsleigh Motor & Marine Engineers Ltd
8, Madeira Avenue, Leigh-on-Sea (Southend 79326)

Diesel Engineers

For navigational information see page following Chart 64.

4 Sea Reach and Medway Channel

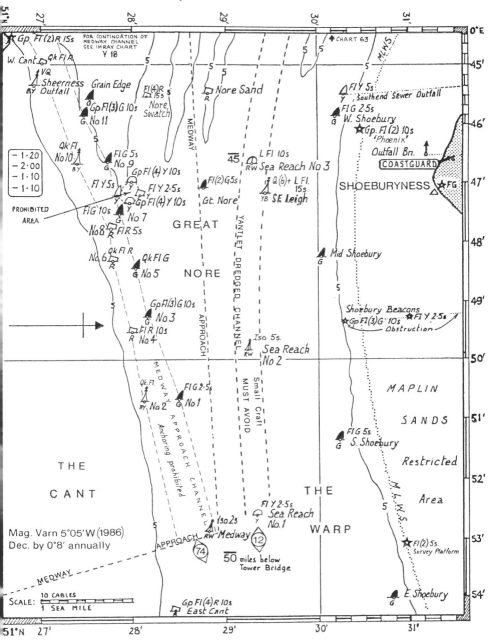

Mag. Varn 5°05'W (1986)
Dec. by 0°8' annually

SCALE: 10 CABLES
1 SEA MILE

Tidal Constants on London Bridge		Mean Tidal Ranges	
HWS — 1hr 20m		Springs	19'0''
LWS — 2hr 00m	at Sheerness (R.Medway)		5.70m
HWN — 1hr 10m		Neaps	15'6''
LWN — 1hr 10m			4.80m

Duration of Rise and Fall of Average Spring and Neap Tides			
Flood		Ebb	
Springs	Neaps	Springs	Neaps
6hrs 00min	6hrs 20min	6hrs 15min	6hrs 15min

CHART DIRECTORY

Thorpe Bay Marine   *Boat sales*
198, Eastern Esplanade, Southend, Essex
(Southend 588065)

Cambridge Service Station   *Fuel supplies (ashore)*
Ness Road, Shoeburyness, Essex
(Shoeburyness 3158/4052)

NAVIGATION NOTES

Note that the tide recedes approximately 1 mile from the shore off Southend. In this area there is a general speed limit of 8 knots (east of a line from Two Tree Island Causeway to the seaward end of Garrison Pier at Shoeburyness; within 600 feet of Southend Pier Head; and within the navigable waters of East Beach, Shoeburyness). Speed should also be kept to a minimum commensurate with maintaining adequate steerage way in all creeks around Canvey Island.

Leigh-on-Sea is only approachable afloat over the flats, two hours either side of High Water, but vessels wishing to lie afloat may moor in Ray Gut over the tide.

Benfleet Creek is best approached from Ray Gut and not by the alternative route via East Haven Creek. Headroom in Benfleet Creek is limited by the flood barrier and the road bridge.

Prior arrangement is advisable for moorings, and should be made with the Pier and Foreshore Office at Pier Hill, Southend. Alternatively, the clubs listed in the Directory on page 195 may be able to allot a mooring to visitors, whom they welcome.

THE CANALS AND LAKES OF THAMESMEAD

Although not connected to the River Thames there is a waterway system in miniature based on the drainage requirements of the new Thamesmead development on the site of Plumstead Marshes between Woolwich and Erith.

At present three lakes are linked by canals. The fourth, and largest lake, Southmere, is available for sailing, windsurfing and canoeing but is not navigably connected to the system. Crossway Lake which is located close to Cross Ness, is linked by means of the Crossway Canal and the Harrow Canal, which runs south-west to the Butts Canal.

This latter canal links the two larger water areas, Thamesmere in the north, close to Barking Reach; and Birchmere in the south. A short arm from Birchmere called the Waterfield Canal, proceeds north-west from it and will eventually be extended westwards to link with Gallions Lake which is yet to be developed, but is shown on Chart 20 north of Gadwall Way. The portion of the old Woolwich Canal still in water has been renamed Broadwater.

The canals are mainly 6 metres wide (20ft approx) although parts of the Crossway and Butts Canals are 9 metres (30ft approx). All have a design depth of 2ft 0in and a standard headroom of 5ft 10in, being designed solely for small craft operating at the discretion of the development authority, mainly canoes. The use of sailing dinghies and sailboards on the lakes is controlled by a system of licensing. Details can be obtained from:

The Recreation and Arts Department
Thamesmead Town, Harrow Manor Way, Thamesmead South, London, SE2 9XH
Tel: 01-310 1500

Technical details:

CROSSWAY CANAL (Crossway Park Weir to Harrow Canal and Crossway Lake)
Length: 780 metres.
Bridges: 5 foot 2 road.
HARROW CANAL (Crossway Canal to Butts Canal)
Length: 1,120 metres.
Bridges: 5 foot 3 road.
BUTTS CANAL (Birchmere to Thamesmere)
Length: 1,080 metres.
Bridges: 3 foot 5 road.
WATERFIELD CANAL (Birchmere to Central Way - not yet completed)
Length: (at March 1986) 300 metres.
Bridges: 1 footbridge.
THAMESMERE, BIRCHMERE AND SOUTHMERE LAKES
Depths: Maximum 2.0 metres (6ft 6in) in centres
            Shore   0.46 metres (1ft 6in) sloping to full depth in approximately
                        13.5 metres (45ft)

The Thamesmead Lakes and Canals

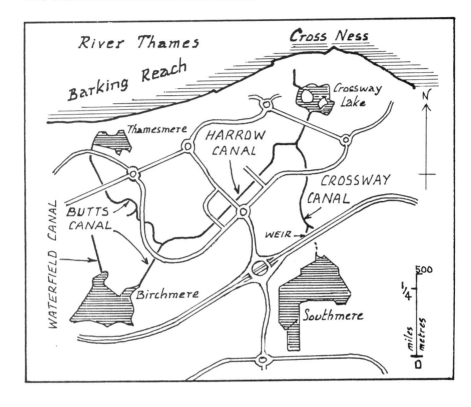

Appendix I

DIRECTIONS AND NOTICES TO THOSE IN CHARGE OF VESSELS ON THE RIVER THAMES, ISSUED BY THE PORT OF LONDON AUTHORITY.

There are certain regulations additional to the International Regulations for Preventing Collisions which require to be observed. Because of the different 'sea-room' available these regulations vary depending on whether navigating above or below London or Tower Bridges.

Above London Bridge

Fairway means the central channel used for navigation up and down the river.

Small Craft means yachts, launches, rowing craft and other small vessels howsoever propelled of less than 20 metres in length.

Vessels means vessels over 20 metres in length.

High Speed Craft means vessels of any length howsoever propelled, capable of proceeding at speeds over 15 knots.

Directions

1. In the fairway, small craft shall not hamper the passage of vessels which can navigate only inside the fairway.

2. Small craft and vessels shall not enter into nor cross the fairway so as to obstruct another vessel proceeding along the fairway.

3. High speed craft shall keep out of the way of all vessels and craft.

4. Vessels in doubt that sufficient action is being taken to avoid collision may indicate this doubt by sounding five or more short and rapid blasts on the whistle.

However, PLA *Notice to Mariners No. 20* of 1984 further requires that:

1. Every vessel of less than 40 metres in length and every sailing vessel is advised, when navigating above Tower Bridge
   a) to treat every vessel of 40 metres or more in length and every vessel engaged in towing as a vessel which can safely navigate only within a narrow channel; and, therefore,
   b) not to impede the passage of that vessel.

2. This advice does not override the requirements of byelaw 17 (1) of the Port of London River Byelaws, 1978. So, where
   (A) a vessel of 40 metres or more in length or a vessel engaged in towing, and
   (B) a vessel of less than 40 metres in length or a sailing vessel
are approaching or passing under a bridge and vessel (A) is navigating against the tide and vessel (B) with the tide, vessel (A) must (in accordance with byelaw 17 (1)) ease her speed and prepare to stop to avoid risk of collision with vessel (B).

Below London Bridge

Fairway means the 1,000 ft wide channel from No. 1 Sea Reach buoy to Graves-end and the main navigational channel from Gravesend to London Bridge. It also means the normal approach to the deep-water anchorages of the Warp and South-end-on-Sea.

Craft means yachts, self-propelled craft and small vessels of any type, howsoever propelled.

Directions

1. In the fairway craft of less than 20 metres in length shall not hamper the passage of a vessel which can navigate only inside the fairway.

2. Craft and vessels shall not enter into nor cross the fairway between No. 1 Sea Reach buoy and London Bridge so as to obstruct another vessel proceeding along the fairway.

3. Outside the fairway, the steering and sailing rules of the International Regulations for Preventing Collisions at Sea and the Port of London River Byelaws, 1978, shall apply, but all craft shall keep well clear of vessels and their attendant tugs which are about to berth or moor.

4. Vessels in doubt that sufficient action is being taken to avoid collision may indicate this doubt by sounding five or more short and rapid blasts on the whistle.

The reader is strongly recommended to purchase a copy of the Port of London River Byelaws, 1978, obtainable from the authority's offices at Thames House, St Andrews Road, Tilbury Docks, Essex, RM18 7JH, if contemplating cruising extensively in the tidal Thames.

NOTICES TO YACHTSMEN ISSUED BY THE PORT OF LONDON AUTHORIT
Public Health, Pollution, etc.

Owners and persons in charge of pleasure craft are reminded that it is an offence punishable on summary conviction by a fine of £500 to throw rubbish (i.e. tins, bottles, cartons, paper, foodstuffs, etc.) or the discharge of any type of toilets into the River Thames.

It is also an offence punishable on summary conviction of a fine of up to £50,00(to spill, discharge or allow to flow into the River Thames any oil, petrol, etc.

There are at several places along the River, barges which are conspicuously marked *Driftwood* into which boat owners are requested to place all non-perishable rubbish, etc.

Appendix II

ADMIRALTY AND IMRAY CHARTS AND CHART AGENTS

Admiralty and Imray Charts of the tidal Thames as covered in this guide are available as follows:

No.	Title
	ADMIRALTY
1185	River Thames – Sea Reach
1186	Tilbury to Canvey
2151	Gallions to Tilbury
2484	Hole Haven to London Bridge
3319	Tower Bridge to Richmond
3337	Tower Bridge to Barking Creek including the Thames Barrier
	IMRAY
C1	The Thames Estuary
C2	River Thames – Teddington to Southend
Y18	River Medway and Approaches

Charts with up-to-date corrections are obtainable from Admiralty appointed Chart Agents. Imray charts are obtainable from most good chandlery stores and bookshops.

Stanfords International Map Centre
12 - 14, Long Acre, London, WC2 (01-836 1321)

Captain O M Watts Ltd
45, Albemarle Street, London, W1X 4BJ (01-493 4633)

J D Potter Limited
145, Minories, London, EC3N 1NH (01-709 9076)

The London Yacht Centre Limited
13, Artillery Lane, Bishopsgate, London, E1 (01-247 0521/9924)

Kelvin Hughes Ltd
31, Mansell Street, London, E1 8AA (01-481 8741)

Brown and Perring Ltd
Redwing House, 36 - 44, Tabernacle Street, London, EC2

Thos. Foulkes
81, Sansom Road, Leytonstone, London, E11 3HB (01-539 5627/5084)

A number of these agents can only hold selected stocks, but will obtain charts to order.

Appendix III

CUSTOMS FORMALITIES and USE OF VHF R/T

If you are using this work of reference prior to a departure from the UK or an arrival in the UK to or from abroad, then you will more than probably require Customs clearance.

On entering United Kingdom territorial waters, a yellow flag, (the "Q" flag in the International Code of Signals), must be flown conspicuously until such time as all customs formalities have been completed. During the hours of darkness the flag should be suitably illuminated.

Notice 8, issued by H M Customs & Excise and obtainable from most local Customs offices, especially those shown in the Directory sections of this guide, sets out the complete details including matters such as Ship's Stores, Immigration, Passports, Light Dues, Charter, Value Added Tax on the vessel, Imports, Prohibited Goods, and Duty-Free Allowances; and the signalling and reporting procedures required before departure and on arrival in UK territorial waters.

Given below is a list, adapted from the latest edition of H M Customs *Notice 8,* of contacts in the Thames estuary area where arrivals and departures should be reported.

GRAVESEND	Custom House GRAVESEND Kent DA12 1BW	01-626 1515 (Ext 5861/5864)
LONDON PORT	Custom House Lower Thames Street LONDON EC3R 6EE	01-626 1515 (Ext 5861/5864)
ROYAL DOCKS (also includes St Katharine Yacht Haven)	No 8 Office Pier Head King George V Dock LONDON E16 2PL	01-626 1515 (Ext 5861/5864)
SOUTHEND-on-SEA	Southend Airport SOUTHEND-on-SEA Essex SS2 6YB	Southend 547141 (Ext 26) or 01-626 1515 (Ext 5861, 5864)
THAMES HAVEN	SFP Admin Building Shell Haven STANFORD-le-HOPE Essex SS17 9LT	01-626 1515 (Ext 5861/5864)

TILBURY DOCK

Tilbury Dock
TILBURY
Essex RM18 7EJ

01-626 1515
(Ext 5861/5864)

In each case if not using VHF R/T Dial 100 and ask for FREEFONE CUSTOMS YACHTS. The correct procedure for notifying Customs of the craft's presence is set out in *Notice 8*. Telephone numbers given above should be called through BTI's Coast Radio Stations, the relevant ones for the Thames being the group comprising Thames, Orfordness and North Foreland, the latter being the controlling station.

North Foreland Radio (Tel: Thanet (0843) 20592)
VHF Wkg Channel: Ch 26   Secondary: Ch 5 and 66 (MF — 1848kHz)

Thames Radio
VHF Wkg Channel: Ch 2   Secondary: Ch 83

Orfordness Radio
VHF Wkg Channel: Ch 62   Secondary: Ch 82

All three stations are now called on their primary working frequencies and not on the Distress/Calling VHF Channel 16.

(The information on radio channels has been supplied by British Telecom International).

Appendix IV

MOORING SITES (Permanent)

Mooring sites for the permanent location of small craft are few and far between in the London Area. Such sites as there are fall into one of three main categories: those administered by the Port of London Authority on the Thames Tideway and those administered by the British Waterways Board on the canal system, which constitute the first; those administered by a lessee boatyard; and thirdly those administered by a recognised cruising or yacht club.

Mooring fees are charged in the first two categories, usually on a quarterly contract (the period recommended by the Ship and Boat Builders' National Federation, as approved by the Royal Yachting Association), but the third category obviously calls for the owner to become a member of the club concerned. However, the club will, no doubt, make additional charges for the use of its mooring facilities.

Details of the mooring facilities available are shown in the chart directories, while a quick reference to the sites is provided in the Location Index under *Mooring Sites.*

Enquiries concerning moorings available from the Port of London Authority or the British Waterways Board should be directed as follows:

Sections 1, 2 and 3
Assistant Harbour Master (Upper); Port of London Authroity, Richmond Lock, Richmond, Surrey (01-940 0634)

Section 4
Assistant Harbour Master (Upper); Port of London Authroity, Tower Pier, London, EC3N 4PL (01-481 0720)

Sections 5 to 8
The Craft Licensing Supervisor (Moorings), British Waterways Board, Willow Grange, Church Road, Watford, Herts, WD1 3QA (Watford 26422)

Section 9
Assistant Harbour Master (Lower), Port of London Authority, Thames Navigation Service, Royal Terrace Pier Road, Gravesend, Kent, DA12 2BG (Gravesend (0474) 67684 or 67655)

Houseboats on the Thames
Houseboats, which are defined as vessels used for residential purposes, are not permitted to moor out in the stream in that part of the river within the jurisdic-

tion of the Port Authority (i.e. downstream from Teddington Lock), and regulations do not allow such craft to berth in any of the Authority's Docks or Basins.

Houseboats may, however, be permitted to berth alongside frontages above Chelsea Bridge, providing always that there is direct access from the shore.

It is necessary in such cases to obtain the permission of the person or firm owning the river frontage, stating that access over their property and the mooring of the vessel at their frontage will be permitted. The agreement of adjacent frontagers is also necessary. The vessel (which it is inadvisable to purchase in anticipation of such permissions) must be inspected to ensure that it is in all respects suitable and riverworthy before proceeding to the site. Additionally it may also be necessary to obtain planning permission.

Appendix V

PASSENGER BOAT DIRECTORY

I am indebted to Geoffrey Hamer, author and publisher of *Trip Out,* a periodical publication listing all kinds of ferry services and pleasure cruises for the British Isles for most of the following information. Copies of *Trip Out* can be obtained from his address given in the Bibliography on page 211.

THAMES TIDEWAY

Bullas Tank Craft Co. **(Greenwich – Barrier Passenger Service)** Telegraph House, Higham, Rochester, Kent (Medway (0634) 717509) **OR** Greenwich Pier, King William Walk, London SE10 9HT (01-858 7150	Greenwich Pier
Campion Launches 41, Speranza Street, London, SE18 1NX (01-854 1842)	Greenwich Pier
Capital Cruises 45a, Heathfield Road, London, SW18 2PH (01-870 7036)	Various piers
Catamaran Cruises West India Dock Pier, Cuba Street, London, E14 8LB (01-987 1185	Various piers
A E Collier 217, St Margarets Road, Twickenham, Mx, TW1 1LU (01-892 0741)	Richmond and Westminster Piers
C R Faldo (WA) 90, Wellington Road, London, E6 2RG (01-471 5772)	Westminster Pier
W Hammerton & Co Ferry Boat House, Marble Hill Park, Twickenham, Mx (01-892 9620)	Hammerton's Ferry
Greenwich, London Borough of, Woolwich Ferry, New Ferry Approach, SE18 6DX (01-854 3488)	Woolwich Free Ferry
W A Jackson (WA) 39, Elmsdale Road, London, E17 6PN (01-520 2090)	Westminster Pier and Richmond L.S.

London Launches   Westminster Pier
4, Vale Grove, London, W3 7QP
(01-740 8263)

Maynard Launches (WA)   Westminster Pier
521, Chessington Road, Epsom, Surrey, KT19 9JB
(01-391 2625)

Meridian Line Cruisers   Greenwich Pier
Greenwich Pier, King William Walk, London, SE10 9HT
(01-858 6895)

S A Metcalf (WA)   Westminster Pier
13, Montague Avenue, London, SE4 1YP
(01-691 1803/01-930 4721)

D G Moore   Westminster Pier
14, Bardell House, Parkers Row, London, SE1 2DH
(01-237 1322)

GHF Parr   Richmond L.S.
15, Albert Road, Teddington, Middx, TW11 0BD
(01-977 2084)

M & CW Phillips (WA)   Westminster Pier
Westminster Pier, Victoria Embankment, London, SW1

W R Pope (WA)   Westminster Pier
Westminster Pier, Victoria Embankment, London, SW1

R G (Passenger Launches)   Ford's Ferry
1, Station Approach, Barnehurst, Bexleyheath, Kent, DA7 6HQ
(Crayford (0322) 524018)

River Functions (Thames) Limited   Cherry Garden Pier
Cherry Garden Pier, Bermondsey Wall East, London, SE16 4TU
(01-237 5134)

River Ride Ltd   Westminster, Festival
Westminster Pier (01-839 3523)   and Charing Cross Piers
Charing Cross Pier (01-930 0970/01-930 8585)
Festival Pier (01-261 0456)

Sargent Brothers (Thames) Ltd   Barrier Gardens Pier
Unity House, Unity Way, SE18 5NL
(01-854 5555)

Thames Launches (WA)   Westminster Pier
Westminster Pier, Victoria Embankment, SW1A 2JH
(01-930 2074)

Thames Pleasure Craft (WA) (TO)   Westminster Pier, Tower Pier
Ivory House, St Katharine-by-the-Tower, E1 9LB   and Greenwich Pier
(01-481 4276)

London's Waterway Guide

Thompson's Launches (WA)
Westminster Pier, Victoria Embankment, SW1A 2JH
(01-930 8589)

Westminster Pier, Tower Pier
and Greenwich Pier

Tidal Cruisers (WA)
47, King Henry's Road, London, NW3 3QR
(01-722 9132)

Westminster Pier, Tower Pier
and Greenwich Pier

Turk Launches
Thames Side, Kingston upon Thames, KT1 1PX
(01-546 2434)

St Helena Pier, Richmond

Westminster Party Boats Ltd
98, Sibthorpe Road, SE12 9DP
(01-857 8938)

Westminster Pier

George Wheeler Launches Ltd (WA)
Westminster Pier, Victoria Embankment, SW1A 2JH
(01-930 4097)

Westminster Pier, Tower Pier
and Greenwich Pier

Wilson's Launches Ltd.
'HMS Belfast'
Symons Wharf, Vine Lane, London, SE1 2JQ
(01-403 4935)

'Belfast' Ferry

Woods River Services Ltd (TO) (WA)
PO Box 177, London, SE3 9JA
(01-481 2711)

Various piers

C H Wyatt (WA)
375, Westborough Road, Westcliff-on-Sea, SS0 9TS
(Southend (0702) 342679)

Westminster Pier and Kew
Gardens Pier

GRAND UNION AND REGENTS CANALS

British Waterways Board
Canal Office, Delamare Terrace, London, W2
(01-286 6101)

Little Venice

Jason's Trip, Barge "Tab"
66, Blomfield Road, London, W9
(01-286 3428)

Little Venice

London Waterbus Co
Camden Lock, Commercial Place, NW1 8AF
(01-485 2550)

Camden Lock

T and D Murrell
Adelaide Dock, Endsleigh Road, Southall, Mx UB2 5QR
(01-848 4485)

Southall & Uxbridge

W E Walker
250 Camden High Street, London, NW1 8QS
(01-485 4433)

Camden Lock

(WA) Member of Westminster Passenger Services Association. (01-930 4097)
(TO) Member, Tower Pier Passenger Launch Operators. (01-488 0344)

Appendix VI

Bibliography

History

Discovering London's Canals Derek Pratt (Shire Publications)
London's Canal (Reprint) Herbert Spencer (Lund Humphries)
Through London By Canal (1885) (Reprint) (British Waterways Board)
On The Canal (1858) J. Hollingshead (British Waterways Board)
London's Waterways Martyn Denney (B. T. Batsford)

Guides

The Ordnance Survey Guide to the Waterways (Robert Nicholson) *Vol 1 South*
The Ordnance Survey Guide to the River Thames (Robert Nicholson)
The Thames Book (Link House Publications)
Inland Waterways of Great Britain and Ireland L. A. Edwards (Imray, Laurie, Norie and Wilson Ltd)
Trip Out (biannually). (Geoffrey Hamer - 77 St Mary's Grove, London, W4 3LW)

Maps and Charts

A–Z Nine-sheet Master Plan of London (Geographer's Map Co. Ltd)
Inland Waterways of England and Wales (Imray, Laurie, Norie and Wilson Ltd)
Charts C1, C2 and Y18 (Imray, Laurie, Norie & Wilson Ltd)

Admiralty Charts
River Thames Charts – 1185, 1186, 2151, 2484, 3319, 3337

Ordnance Survey Maps
1:50.000 – Sheets 166, 167, 176, 177, 178

Appendix VII

CLASSIFIED LIST OF USEFUL ADDRESSES

ACCIDENT PREVENTION
Royal Life Saving Society, 14 Devonshire Street, London, W1.
Royal Society for the Prevention of Accidents, Royal Oak Centre, Brighton Road, Purley, Surrey, CR2 2UR

ANGLING
London Anglers' Association, Forest Road Hall, Hervey Park Road, London, E17 7LJ
Thames Water Authority, Nugent House, Vastern Road, Reading, RG1 8DB
The Fisheries Officer, British Waterways Board, Willow Grange, Church Road, Watford, Herts, WD1 3QA

ASSOCIATIONS
Association of Thames Yacht Clubs, 4, Plough Close, Shillingford, Oxfordshire.
Association of Waterways Cruising Clubs, 21 – 29, Hazlewood Road, Northampton, NN1 1LB
British Canoe Union, 70 Brompton Road, London, SW3.
Inland Waterways Association, 114 Regent's Park Road, London, NW1 8UQ
River Thames Society, 2, Chestnut Lodge Cottages, Old Common Road, Cobham, Surrey, KT11 1BU
Royal Yachting Association, Victoria Way, Woking, Surrey, GU21 1EQ
Ship and Boat Builders' National Federation, Boating Industry House, Vale Road, Weybridge, Surrey, KT13 9NS

BOAT SAFETY
Department of Trade and Industry, Gaywood House, Great Peter Street, London, SW1P 3LV

BOAT CONSTRUCTION INFORMATION
Lloyds Register of Shipping, 71 Fenchurch Street, London, EC3M 4BS
Ship and Boat Builders' National Federation, Boating Industry House, Vale Road, Weybridge, Surrey, KT13 9NS

CHARTS
British Waterways Board, Melbury House, Melbury Terrace, London, NW1 6JX
Hydrographic Department. Ministry of Defence, Taunton, Somerset.
Port of London Authority, Hydrographic Officer, Thames Navigation Service, Royal Terrace Pier Road, Gravesend, Kent, DA12 2BG
Imray, Laurie, Norie and Wilson Ltd, Wych House, St Ives, Huntingdon, Cambs.

COASTGUARD SERVICE
HM Coastguard/Department of Trade, Sunley House, High Holborn, London, WC1

CUSTOMS & EXCISE
HM Customs and Excise, CDE1, Dorset House, Stamford Street, London, SE1 9PS

GOVERNMENT (Central and Local) SPONSORED AMENITY ORGANISATIONS
English Tourist Board, 4 Grosvenor Gardens, London, SW1
Lea Valley Regional Park Authority, Myddelton House, Bulls Cross, Enfield, Middx.
London Tourist Board, 26, Grosvenor Gardens, London, SW1
Inland Waterways Amenity Advisory Committee, 122, Cleveland Street, London, W1P 5DN
London, NW1 6JX

MERCHANT SHIPPING NOTICES
Department of Trade and Industry, Eileen House, 80–94 Newington Causeway, London,
SE1 6DD

METEOROLOGICAL INFORMATION
The Secretary, **Meteorological Office,** Eastern Road, Bracknell, Berks, RG12 2UR

NAVIGATION AUTHORITIES
British Waterways Board, Melbury House, Melbury Terrace, London, NW1 6JX
Dartford and Crayford Navigation Commissioners, Dartford Lock, Dartford, Kent
National Trust (Wey and Godalming Navigations), Dapdune Wharf, Dapdune Lea,
Woodbridge Road, Guildford, Surrey
Port of London Authority, World Trade Centre, London, E19AA
Thames Water Authority, Nugent House, Vastern Road, Reading, Berks, RG1 8DB

PUBLICATIONS
British Waterways Board, Melbury House, Melbury Terrace, London, NW1 6JX
HM Stationery Office, 49 High Holborn, London, WC1
Inland Waterways Association, 114 Regents Park Road, London, NW1 8UQ
Thames Information Service. Gresham House, Twickenham Road, Feltham, Middx,
TW13 6HA
Waterways World Book Service, Kottingham House, Dale Street, Burton-on-Trent, Staffs,
DE14 3TD

RADIO LICENSING
Home Office Licensing, Radio Regulatory Division, Waterloo Bridge House, Waterloo
Road, London, SE1 8UA

RADIO SERVICES FOR YACHTSMEN
British Telecom International, Maritime Radio Services, 1st Floor, 43, Bartholomew
Close, London, EC1A 7HP

REGISTRATION (DTI)
The Registrar, London Custom House, Port of London, Lower Thames Street, London,
EC3R 6EE
The Registrar General of Shipping and Seamen, Llantrisant Road, Llandaff, Cardiff.

REGISTRATION (Lloyds)
Lloyds Register of Shipping, 71 Fenchurch Street, London, EC3M 4BS

TRADING
London Port Promotion Association, Tilbury Docks, Essex, RM18 7EH
Inland Shipping Group, (IWA) 114, Regent's Park Road, London, NW1 8UQ
Thames Passenger Services Federation, Tamesis House, 9, Wapping Lane, London, E1 9DA

Appendix VIII
USEFUL CONVERSION TABLES

IMPERIAL/METRIC – METRIC/IMPERIAL CONVERSION TABLES in linear measure and speed conversion

Metric measurements have been taken to two decimal places except in the Depth Tables which relate to soundings on charts, which are normally shown to the nearest metre (metric) or fathom (imperial).

Ft.	Ins.	Metres	Ft.	Ins.	Metres	Metres	Ft.	Ins.	Fathoms	Metres	SPEEDS	
											Knots	M.P.H.
—	¼	0.01	7	—	2.12	0.25	—	9	½	1	1	1.2
—	½	0.01	8	—	2.41	0.50	1	9	1	2	2	2.3
—	¾	0.02	9	—	2.74	0.75	2	6	2	4	3	3.5
—	1	0.03	10	—	3.05	1.00	3	3	3	5	4	4.6
—	2	0.05	11	—	3.35	1.50	5	0	4	7	5	5.7
—	3	0.08	12	—	3.66	2.00	6	6	5	9	6	6.9
—	4	0.10	13	—	3.96	2.50	8	3	10	18	7	8.1
—	5	0.13	14	—	4.27	3.00	9	9	20	37	8	9.2
—	6	0.15	15	—	4.57	4.00	13	0			9	10.4
—	7	0.18	20	—	6.10	5.00	16	6			10	11.6
—	8	0.20	25	—	7.62	6.00	19	9	Metres	*Feet/*		
—	9	0.23	30	—	9.14	7.00	23	0		Fathoms		
—	10	0.25	35	—	10.67	8.00	26	3	½	2 or ¼		
—	11	0.28	40	—	12.19	9.00	29	6	1	3 or ½		
1	0	0.31	45	—	13.72	10.00	33	0	2	1		
1	3	0.38	50	—	15.24	11.00	36	3	3	1½		
1	6	0.46	60	—	18.29	12.00	39	6	4	2		
1	9	0.53	70	—	21.34	13.00	42	6	5	3		
2	0	0.61	80	—	24.38	14.00	46	0	10	5½		
2	3	0.69	90	—	27.43	15.00	49	3	20	11		
2	6	0.76	100	—	30.48	20.00	66	6	30	16		
2	9	0.84	150	—	45.72	30.00	98	0				
3	0	0.91	200	—	60.96	40.00	131	0				
4	0	1.22	250	—	76.20	50.00	164	0				
5	0	1.52	300	—	91.44	100.00	328	0				
6	0	1.83	350	—	106.68	200.00	654	0				

Note: In the two main tables Imperial measure in excess of 1 foot is given to the nearest 3 inches up to 20 metres and

Appendix IX

TABLES OF DISTANCES

Distances shown in Statute Land Miles to two decimal places.

Downstream	RIVER THAMES	Upstream
0.00	Teddington Barge Lock (tail)	68.92
3.16	Richmond Lock	65.76
5.01	Grand Union Canal Entrance	63.91
16.80	Westminster Bridge	52.12
18.69	London Bridge	50.23
21.09	Regent's Canal Entrance	47.83
23.15	Deptford Creek	45.77
25.69	Bow Creek	43.23
27.21	Thames Barrier	41.71
30.06	Margaret Ness (Tripcock Point)	38.86
36.53	Crayford Ness	32.39
41.73	Broad Ness	27.19
45.35	Gravesend, Royal Terrace Pier	23.57
50.55	Lower Hope Point	18.37
61.95	Southend Pier	6.97
68.92	Sea Reach Buoy No. 1	0.00
	GRAND UNION CANAL (MAIN LINE)	
0.00	Springwell Lock No. 83	17.47
5.25	Uxbridge Lock No. 88	12.22
7.81	Cowley Peachey Junction	9.66
11.47	Bulls Bridge Junction	6.00
14.44	Hanwell Bottom Lock No. 97	3.03
17.47	Brentford – Junction with River Thames	0.00
	GRAND UNION CANAL (PADDINGTON ARM)	
0.00	Bulls Bridge Junction with main line	12.94
8.06	North Circular Road Aqueduct	4.88
12.94	Little Venice – Junction with Regent's Canal	0.00
13.56	Paddington Basin	0.62
	REGENT'S CANAL	
0.00	Little Venice – Junction with Paddington Arm	8.62
2.25	Hampstead Road Locks No. 1	6.37
3.75	West End of Islington Tunnel	4.87
6.87	Hertford Union Junction, Old Ford	1.75
8.37	Commercial Road Lock No. 12	0.25
8.62	Limehouse Ship Lock No. 13 – River Thames	0.00
	LEE NAVIGATION	
0.00	Waltham Town Lock No. 11	14.81
7.00	Tottenham Lock No. 17	7.81
9.25	Lea Bridge	5.56
11.12	Hackney Junction with Hertford Union Canal	3.69

12.81	Bow Tidal Locks No. 20	2.00
14.31	Limehouse Basin (via Limehouse Cut)	(1.50)
14.81	Bow Creek Mouth (River Thames)	0.00
	HERTFORD UNION CANAL	
0.00	Old Ford Junction – Regent's Canal	1.19
1.19	Hackney Junction, Lee Navigation	0.00

Gazetteer

The numbers in italics immediately following each entry refer to the charts on which the features will be found. Page references follow.

All known alternative names have been indexed and cross-referenced in the Gazetteer although for reasons of clarity in some cases only the more usual name is shown on the actual chart.

Subject Index

All geographical locations will be found in the Gazetteer. Inns and restaurants, etc. are listed in the separate index on page

Port of London Authority 11–20, 35, 53, 67, 68, 70, 77, 78, 82–84, 180, 190
Practical navigation 2–3, 92–93, 109, 143–145, 154–155, 181, 187–188, 193, 198
Publications 211

Radio – see 'Marine radio (VHF)' above
Railways – see 'British Rail' or 'London Regional Transport' or 'Docklands Light Railway' in this index. Individual stations by name will be found in the gazetteer.
Refuse disposal 28, 31, 36, 43, 51, 57, 58, 67, 95, 100, 101, 113, 119, 131, 132, 167, 172, 174
Repairers 28, 31, 35, 36, 39, 43, 45, 47, 67, 73, 75, 77, 96, 100, 101, 113, 167, 172, 174, 184, 191, 195, 196
Rise, of locks – see under 'Fall, of locks'
Rivers 1, 2, 9–85, 149–176, 177–198
River Police 43, 57, 67, 139, 159, 186
Rubbish, floating 3, 51, 155

Sailing 13, 47, 199
Sanitary stations 7, 28, 31, 36, 58, 67, 95, 100, 101, 104, 113, 119, 132, 137, 174
Sound signals 13, 14, 51, 70–71
Speed limits 13, 23, 41, 48, 49, 91, 123
Sunken craft 15
Swimming (prohibited in canals) 124

Taxi cabs 6, 7
Telephones 7
Tidal constants, duration and set 28, 31, 35, 36, 39, 43, 45, 47, 49, 53, 55, 57, 61, 67, 73, 75, 77, 78, 95, 159, 183, 186, 188, 193, 195, 198

Tidal working 24–28
Thames Water Authority:
Lea Division 152, 154, 159
Navigation Service (Upper Thames) 23
Tideway Group 11, 35, 39, 46, 47, 56, 57, 58, 65, 66, 67, 74, 75, 79, 82
Towing paths 21, 31, 32, 35, 39, 43, 45, 47, 49, 93, 101, 104, 113, 119, 123, 124, 132, 137, 156, 159, 174
Tunnels, canal, 88, 116, 123, 125, 129, 133, 134
Tunnels, rail, 54, 56, 60, 66, 116, 125, 129, 134, 138
Tunnels, road, 72, 76, 138, 158, 185

Underground railways – see under 'London Regional Transport'

Water points 28, 29, 30, 31, 34, 35, 36, 37, 38, 39, 42, 43, 44, 45, 46, 47, 56, 57, 58, 66, 67, 94, 95, 98, 99, 100, 101, 103, 104, 111, 113, 116, 119, 125, 129, 131, 132, 134, 135, 137, 138, 139, 166, 167, 172, 174, 184, 190, 195
Water ski-ing 13
Waterway authorities 213
Wrecks and obstructions (Thames) 14

Index of Hotels, Restaurants and Inns

This is not an exhaustive list but shows the establishments which have easy access to the waterways, or have a connection therewith, by name, decor or ownership. *Those marked with an asterisk are afloat. †Those marked with a dagger operate while cruising.